寿司ペディアTOKYO
早川 光

The Best 12 Affordable
Sushi Restaurants
in Tokyo
by Hikari Hayakawa

江戸前寿司。
その江戸　　　　　　　　　　　　　早川光が自ら名店をセレクト。
1月から12月まで、その月を代表する5貫＋マグロ1貫の寿司だねを「いま食べるべき旬」
として紹介します！

INTRODUCTION

Edomae sushi, one of various sushi styles in Japan, is the art of "food" and a treasure of Japan you can find all over the world nowadays.

Hikari Hayakawa, writer also known as sushi specialist, welcomes you to the amazing world of Edomae sushi featuring five pieces of nigiri and one maguro nigiri from the finest sushi restaurants of his choice every month from January to December, giving you guide to "what to eat in season".

CONTENTS

はじめに　INTRODUCTION…1　　目次　CONTENTS…2・3
著者紹介　About the author…4

1月の寿司　Sushi in January …5

ヒラメ　Japanese Flatfish ／赤貝　Red Clam ／サワラ　Spanish Mackerel…6・7
サヨリ　Japanese Halfbeak ／トラフグの白子　Milt of Japanese Puffer ／1月のマグロ Tuna…8・9
1月の名店　銀座『すし佐竹』　January 〜 Sushi Satake, Ginza…10

2月の寿司　Sushi in February …11

カスゴ　Baby Sea Bream ／アジ　Horse Mackerel ／サクラマス　Cherry Salmon…12・13
カキ　Oyster ／ムラサキウニ　Purple Sea Urchin ／2月のマグロ Tuna…14・15
2月の名店　西麻布『鮨 麻葉』　　February 〜 Sushi Asaba, Nishiazabu…16

3月の寿司　Sushi in March …17

タイ　Sea Bream ／シラウオ　Icefish ／アオヤギ　Surf Clam…18・19
ミル貝　Horse Clam ／ハマグリ　Hard Clam ／3月のマグロ Tuna…20・21
3月の名店　東日本橋『鮨 一條』　　March 〜 Sushi Ichijo, Higashi-Nihombashi…22

4月の寿司　Sushi in April …23

カツオ　Bonito ／アサリ　Japanese Littleneck Clam ／シロイカ　Swordtip Squid…24・25
シロエビ　Broad Velvet Shrimp ／トリ貝　Japanese Cockle ／4月のマグロ Tuna…26・27
4月の名店　湯島『鮨 真菜』　April 〜 Sushi Mana, Yushima…28

5月の寿司　Sushi in May …29

マコガレイ Marbled Sole ／イサキ Grunt ／毛ガニ Horsehair Crab…30・31
アオリイカ Bigfin Reef Squid ／コハダ Midium-sized Konoshiro Gizzard Shad ／
5月のマグロ Tuna …32・33
5月の名店　六本木『鮨 由う』　May 〜 Sushi YUU, Roppongi…34

6月の寿司　Sushi in June …35

アワビ　Abalone ／ホシガレイ Spotted Halibut ／クルマエビ Japanese Tiger Prawn…36・37
アナゴ Sea Eel ／アユ Sweetfish ／6月のマグロ Tuna…38・39
6月の名店　浅草『鮨 久いち』　　June 〜 Sushi Hisaichi, Asakusa…40

7 月の寿司　Sushi in July …41

アカアマダイ Red Tilefish ／キンメダイ Splendid Alfonsino ／
シンコ Baby Konoshiro Gizzard Shad…42・43
煮ダコ Simmered Octopus ／シロイカ Swordtip Squid ／7 月のマグロ Tuna…44・45
7 月の名店　銀座『鎌倉 以ず美 ginza』　　July 〜 Kamakura Izumi ginza, Ginza…46

8 月の寿司　Sushi in August …47

イワシ Sardine ／シマアジ Striped Jack ／キス Whiting…48・49
キジハタ Red Spotted Grouper ／ウニ四種盛り Sea Urchin ／8 月のマグロ Tuna…50・51
8 月の名店　四谷荒木町『鮨わたなべ』　　August 〜 Sushi Watanabe, Yotsuya-Arakicho…52

9 月の寿司　Sushi in September …53

イクラ Salmon Roe ／イカウニ Squid and Sea Urchin ／サンマ Pacific Saury …54・55
タイのあん肝乗せ　Sea Bream with Monkfish Liver Topping ／
カマス Barracuda ／9 月のマグロ Tuna…56・57
9 月の名店　目黒『鮨 りんだ』　　September 〜 Sushi RINDA, Meguro …58

10 月の寿司 Sushi in October …59

ブリ Yellowtail ／シラカワ White Tilefish ／ハマグリ Hard Clam…60・61
サバの棒寿司 Rod-shaped Mackerel Sushi ／
タイラ貝 Japanese Pen Shell ／10 月のマグロ Tuna…62・63
10 月の名店　銀座『鮨 鈴木』　　October 〜 Sushi Suzuki, Ginza…64

11 月の寿司　Sushi in November …65

アナゴ Sea eel ／カジキ Striped Marlin ／
スミイカ Japanese Spineless Cuttlefish…66・67
サバ Mackerel ／戻りガツオ Bonito Returning to the South ／11 月のマグロ Tuna…68・69
11 月の名店　人形町『㐂寿司』　　November 〜 Kizushi, Ningyo-cho…70

12 月の寿司　Sushi in December …71

ミズダコ Giant Pacific Octopus ／カワハギ Thread-sail Filefish ／
キハダマグロ Yellowfin Tuna…72・73
北寄貝 Surf Clam ／ノドグロ Rosy Seabass ／12 月のマグロ Tuna…74・75
12 月の名店　阿佐ヶ谷『鮨なんば 阿佐ヶ谷』　　December 〜 Sushi Namba, Asagaya…76

寿司用語　Sushi Terms …77

早川　光

3月20日生まれ、東京都新宿区出身。著述家、漫画原作者。

『鮨水谷の悦楽』『日本一江戸前鮨がわかる本』など江戸前寿司に関する著書多数。

漫画原作者としては『江戸前鮨職人きららの仕事』『ごほうびおひとり鮨』などのヒット作を持つ。

BS12の寿司番組『早川光の最高に旨い寿司』のナビゲーターとしても活躍。

Hikari Hayakawa

Writer born in Tokyo on March 20. Has various works on Edomae sushi, also famous for writing original stories for sushi manga. Hosts TV show about sushi at BS12.

竹内香苗

9月14日生まれ、愛知県出身。翻訳＆英訳。

東京外国語大学外国語学部卒業。元TBSアナウンサー。

実用英語技能検定試験1級。国際連合公用英語検定試験特A級。

Kanae Takeuchi

Former TBS announcer born in Nagoya on September 14. Graduated from Tokyo University of Foreign Studies.English Translation.

睦月 [1月] の寿司
About Sushi in January
寿司だねの特徴

豊洲市場の初セリから始まる江戸前寿司の1月（睦月）。日本近海の海水温が1年のうちで最も下がる時期だけに、どの魚も身にたっぷりと脂を貯えています。
その中でも旬のピークを迎えるのがヒラメとブリ。いずれもこの時期に獲れるものだけが「寒ビラメ」「寒ブリ」と呼ばれ、最上級の扱いを受けます。
もちろん、江戸前寿司の主役であるマグロにも極上の脂がのっています。ただし最も有名なマグロの産地である青森県大間のホンマグロ漁は例年1月半ばには漁期を終えてしまうので、この1月がシーズンの最後ということになります。

JANUARY

In January, traditionally called "Mutsuki", the first auction of the year is held at Toyosu Market. Every fish is loaded with fat around this time when the sea temperature around Japan is at the lowest throughout the year.
Among which, hirame (Japanese flatfish) and buri (yellowtail) are at their best. Only those caught in this season are called by special names "kan-birame" (winter Japanese flatfish) and "kan-buri" (winter yellowtail), to be treated exceptionally.
Of course, you can also enjoy the finest fat of maguro (tuna), the king of Edomae sushi. However, January is at the end of the season for maguro since the fishing season is over by the middle of this month around Oma in Aomori Prefecture, famous for the best maguro.

Sushi Satake, Ginza

睦月　第1貫

ヒラメ　Hirame (Japanese Flatfish)

Kan-birame of Aomori is best in January

Hirame is a major white fish in Edomae sushi, and lives in the wide range of area from Hokkaido all the way down to the southern part of Japan, Kyushu. They are popularly farmed and seen all year round but the most delicious are, without a doubt, the non-farmed. Especially "kan-birame" that appears in the coldest January to February is famous for the excellent taste. Kan-birame caught in the cold sea of Aomori is the master's choice.
"Kan-birame of Aomori is beyond delicious in January. They are just the best. Not only the fat is tasty, but also the quality is high. And the meat is thick, so the balance with the rice is very nice when made into nigiri, looking beautifully," says Mr. Takeshi Satake, the master of Sushi Satake.
The fat of hirame melts slowly and elegantly in the mouth, soft but not too soft, sweet and savory. You might even notice the sweetness change as you chew.

青森の寒ビラメは1月がベスト

ヒラメは江戸前寿司を代表する白身魚。北海道から九州まで幅広く生息し、養殖も盛んに行われているので、市場には一年中流通していますが、最も美味とされるのは冬の天然物。とりわけ1〜2月の厳冬の時期に獲れる「寒ビラメ」の美味しさには定評があります。
『すし佐竹』の親方・佐竹大さんが選んだのも、青森の極寒の海で獲れた寒ビラメです。
「青森の寒ビラメは旨い。特に1月がベスト。てっぺんだと思います。ただ脂がのっているというだけじゃなくて、脂の質が高い。しかも身に厚みがあるので、握りにした時にシャリとのバランスがよく、美しく仕上がるんです」
握りを食べると、ヒラメの脂がゆっくりと融け、上品な甘みが舌に伝わります。噛めば柔らかさの中にしなやかな弾力があり、噛みしめるほどに甘みが深い旨みへと変わっていきます。

睦月　第2貫

赤貝　Akagai (Red Clam)

The fresh flavor of akagai from Yuriage

There are many kinds of clams made into nigiri sushi, such as mirugai (horse clam), torigai (Japanese cockle), hokkigai (surf clam), to name a few, and winter is the best season for akagai (red clam).
Mutsu Bay of Aomori Prefecture and Mikawa Bay of Aichi Prefecture are well known for good akagai but Mr. Satake prefers Yuriage in Miyagi Prefecture.
"I believe Yuriage is number one. The clams are thicker, tastier, and the flavor is exceptional. But the flavor soon deceases once out of the shell, so I take out on the day we use them."
The aroma of fresh akagai is as fresh as fruits. You will enjoy every crispy bite. Sweet flavor of the juicy meat harmonizes with the sourness of vinegared rice.

閖上の赤貝の魅力は爽やかな香り

ミル貝、トリ貝、北寄貝など江戸前寿司ではさまざまな種類の貝を握りますが、冬に旬を迎えるのは赤貝です。
産地としては青森県の陸奥湾、愛知県の三河湾などが知られていますが、佐竹さんは宮城県閖上産の赤貝を握ります。
「僕は閖上が一番だと思います。他の産地のものに比べて肉厚で甘みもあるし、ずば抜けて香りがいいんです。赤貝の香りは殻から剥いて時間が経つとどんどん失われてしまいますから、必ず握る当日に剥くようにしています」
新鮮な赤貝の香りはフルーツのように爽やか。身はサクッと歯切れがよく、みずみずしいのが特徴。そして優しい甘さが辛口のシャリとよく合います。

サワラ
Sawara (Spanish Mackerel)

"Spring fish" but January is the best season

Sawara (Spanish mackerel) is not so well known around Tokyo but very popular in the west part of Japan, especially in Okayama where one third of all the catch in Japan is consumed. But it has become known nationwide in the recent years that more Edomae sushi restaurants use it. Mr. Satake finds a great value in sawara for sushi.
"In winter, sawara becomes soft and it's perfect for sushi. When you write sawara in kanji (Chinese characters), it signifies "spring fish" but the best time to enjoy is winter, at their fattest. I lightly grill them before making nigiri. This way, they become super soft and fluffy even."
Grilling lightly makes the skin of sawara crispy and the tempting aroma induces your appetite. Once in the mouth, you may feel the piece of fish embraces your tongue.

魚へんに春と書くが、旨いのは1月

サワラは関東地方では馴染みが薄く、関西以西で愛されている魚です。特に岡山では人気が高く、全国で水揚げされたサワラの約3割が岡山県で消費されるのだとか。近年になってその魅力が全国的に知られるようになり、江戸前の寿司屋でも使う所が増えてきました。
佐竹さんも寿司だねとしてのサワラを高く評価しています。
「冬のサワラは身が柔らかいので寿司に合います。"鰆"という漢字は魚へんに春ですけど、サワラが本当に美味しいのは脂がのる冬だと思います。うちでは握りにする前に皮を軽く火で炙るんですが、こうすると身が膨らんでふわふわの食感になるんです」
火で炙ることで皮はパリパリになり、芳ばしい香りが食欲をそそります。食べれば、膨らんだ身が舌を優しく包むかのように感じます。

Sushi Satake, Ginza

睦月　第4貫

サヨリ
Sayori (Japanese Halfbeak)

Using tatejio to bring out the potential

Sayori (Japanese halfbeak) is one of the classic ingredients for Edomae sushi with its beautiful, semitransparent meat and shimmering silver skin. It has an impression as summer fish from the refreshing appearance but the best season is from winter to early spring.
"Sayori has a light taste but more fat and taste in winter than in summer. Dehydrating the meat with salt brings out more of its flavor. However, we don't sprinkle salt but soak in strong saline water to avoid unevenness."
Also, when removing skin of sayori, Mr. Satake leaves a little in the middle. This makes sayori look even more beautiful.

たて塩を使って美味しさを引き出す

美しい半透明の身と光沢のある銀皮が印象的なサヨリは、江戸前寿司には欠かせない魚のひとつ。その涼しげな見た目から夏の魚というイメージがありますが、旬は冬から早春にかけてです。
「淡白な味の魚ですが、夏よりは冬の方が脂があるし、旨みもあります。水分が多い魚なのでひと塩あてて脱水することでさらに旨みが立ってきます。ただしサヨリの場合は振り塩では味にむらが出来てしまうので、たて塩という濃い塩水を使って塩じめします」
佐竹さんはサヨリの皮を引く時に、真ん中だけ銀皮が残るように工夫しています。こうすることで、サヨリの美しさをさらに際立たせているのです。

睦月　第5貫

トラフグの白子
Torafugu Shirako (Milt of Japanese Puffer)

Shirako of the highest quality fugu is thick and creamy

Fugu (pufferfish) is very popular as an ingredient for Japanese hot pot or sashimi in the western part of Japan. There are many kinds such as kusafugu, gomafugu, and shousaifugu, but torafugu (Japanese pufferfish) is considered the highest rank.
Not only the meat but also shirako (milt) of torafugu is very delicious. Especially, a gourmet would drool over winter shirako fully nourished for spring spawning season.
"I also use shirako of mafugu or gomafugu but torafugu definitely stands out as for the taste. It is way beyond others. By grilling until the skin turns golden brown, it becomes so creamy inside like white sauce and you can enjoy rich butter-like taste."
Mr. Satake does not serve shirako as ordinary nigiri sushi, but puts grilled shirako on top of sushi rice in a small bowl. Break the shirako with spoon and mix with vinegared rice below, you will enjoy the finest crème risotto.

最高級フグの白子はとろとろでクリーミー

鍋や刺身の材料として西日本で親しまれているフグ。クサフグ、ゴマフグ、ショウサイフグなど多くの種類がある中で、最高級の評価をされているのがトラフグです。
そしてトラフグは身ばかりでなく、白子も非常に美味。特に春の産卵期に備えて栄養を蓄えた真冬の白子は食通たちの垂涎の的となっています。
「マフグやゴマフグの白子も使いますが、味はトラフグがダントツ。レベルが違います。皮に焼き目がつくまで炙ると中がとろとろのホワイトソースのようになって、旨みも甘さもぐっと濃厚になる。これはもう最高です」
握りではなく、炙った白子をシャリの上に乗せ、小さな丼にして出すのが佐竹さんのスタイル。添えられたスプーンで白子を崩し、シャリと混ぜて食べれば、まるで極上のクリームリゾットのような味わいが楽しめます。

銀座 『すし佐竹』

睦月のマグロ（霜降り）
January Maguro (Shimofuri)

The ultimate otoro, aged for 10 days

Maguro (tuna) is the number one specialty. It is the symbol and a must-have of Edomae sushi. It is said that the level of maguro served determines the status of the restaurant, so masters of top-class sushi restaurants select the best maguro with pride.
This day, Mr. Satake used hon-maguro (bluefin tuna) from the Tsugaru Strait famous for the best maguro around Japan. Moreover, it was the ultimate otoro carved from "harakami", extra fatty part of belly, which hit the highest price among the other parts.
"This is otoro called 'shimofuri.' This shimofuri becomes tastier and softer by aging in the refrigerator so I let them rest for about 10 days".
When Mr. Satake makes otoro nigiri, he makes the sushi rice hotter than for other kinds of fish.
"I've never taken the temperature with a thermometer, but sushi rice is commonly made around 40℃ , this may be about 50℃ ."
Otoro's fat melts on hot ball of rice in a second due to its low melting point, covering the tongue like juice. That is, a special moment you can only experience here.

10日間熟成させた、究極の大トロ

マグロは"寿司屋の看板"。江戸前寿司にはなくてはならない象徴のような存在です。どんなマグロを置いているかでその店の格が決まるとまで言われていますから、一流と呼ばれる店の親方は、プライドを賭けて最高のマグロを手に入れるのです。
この日佐竹さんが握ったマグロは、日本近海の産地ではトップとされる津軽海峡で獲れたホンマグロ。しかもマグロの部位の中で最も高価で取り引きされる"腹カミ"のブロックから切り分けた、究極の大トロです。
「これは"霜降り"と呼ばれる大トロ。この霜降りは冷蔵庫で熟成させることで美味しくなり、食感も柔らかくなるので、だいたい10日間くらい寝かしています」
そして佐竹さんが大トロを握る時は、シャリを通常の温度よりかなり高めに調節します。
「温度計で計ったことはありませんが、普通のシャリが40℃前後だとしたら、50℃くらいはあると思います」
この熱々のシャリによって、融点の低い大トロの脂が一瞬にして蕩け、そのままジュースのように舌を覆い尽くすのです。それはまさにこの店でしか体験できない至福の瞬間です。

Sushi Satake, Ginza

銀座 『すし佐竹』

親方の佐竹大（たけし）さんは銀座の「すし乾山」や「久兵衛」で修業した気鋭の鮨職人。豊洲市場で吟味した最高の素材を揃えているのはもちろん、それぞれの素材に合わせてシャリの温度を調整して握るという新しいスタイルで注目を集めている。

住所：東京都中央区銀座 8-18-16
電話：03-6775-3878
営業時間：【昼】 12：00～14：00（L.O）
　　　　　【夜】 17：00～22：00（L.O）
定休日：不定休（主に日曜日休み）
HP：https://sushi-satake.com/
FB：https://www.facebook.com/sushisatake/

Sushi Satake, Ginza

The master of Sushi Satake, Mr. Takeshi Satake, is a spirited master of sushi, trained at Sushi Kenzan and Kyubei in Ginza. Not to mention his extraordinary sense in selecting the best ingredients at Toyosu Market, the new style of adjusting the temperature of sushi rice for each piece of fish as he makes in his hand is attracting sushi lovers.

Address：8-18-16, Ginza, Chuo-ku, Tokyo　Tel：03-6775-3878
Open：【lunch】12：00～14：00（L.O）【dinner】17：00～22：00（L.O）
Closed：Occasionally（Mainly Sundays）
HP：https://sushi-satake.com/
FB：https://www.facebook.com/sushisatake/

About Sushi in February
如月
[2月]
の寿司
寿司だねの特徴

如月（2月）は季節の上では冬ですが、江戸前寿司では脂をたっぷり貯えた冬の魚と、春を先取りした"走り"の魚が共存する時期にあたります。

冬の寿司だねの中で2月に最も美味しくなるのはサバとカキ。どちらも秋のイメージが強いのですが、真冬のサバは秋よりさらに脂がのり、カキも冬の方が濃厚な味わいになります。

マグロは青森県の大間や三厩など津軽海峡での漁が終わり、漁場が日本海へと移ってきます。魚体の大きさは餌の豊富な津軽海峡に及ばなくても、冬のマグロですから脂はしっかりのっています。

February, traditionally called "Kisaragi", is still winter but in the world of Edomae sushi it is the period in which fatty winter fish and some early spring fish coexist.
The best ingredients for sushi in February are saba (mackerel) and kaki (oyster). Despite the autumn image they may have, saba carries more fat in midwinter than in fall and kaki has richer taste in winter.
As for maguro (tuna), the fishing season ends around Minmaya and Oma in the Tsugaru Strait that connects the Sea of Japan and the Pacific Ocean, and the fishing area moves down west to the Sea of Japan. Although the size of maguro is smaller than those more nourished in the Tsugaru Strait, the winter maguro is still fatty enough.

FEBRUARY

Sushi Asaba, Nishiazabu

如月　第1貫

カスゴ　Kasugo (Baby Sea Bream)

Dressed with savor of aged kombu

Young fish of tai (sea bream) including madai (red sea bream), kidai (yellowback sea bream), and chidai (crimson sea bream), about 10cm is called "kasugo".
Kasugo is considered as spring fish for it is written "spring baby" in Chinese characters but it has no specific season because the fish is in the middle of growth. However, the meat of winter kasugo is thicker and tastier than the summer one.
The master of Sushi Asaba, Mr. Naoya Hanawa, prefers using winter kasugo. "I use spring kasugo also but winter kasugo is softer so it is good for nigiri. The fish having subtle flavor, I cure them with kombu (kelp) so that the meat absorbs the good flavor of kombu and to bring out a little sweetness."
Mr. Hanawa uses makombu (a kind of kombu) matured for five years. The taste of the cured fish is so profound and rich that you might not believe they are little baby sea bream.

5年熟成の昆布の旨みを纏わせる

江戸前寿司では体長10センチ程度のタイ（マダイ、キダイ、チダイ）の幼魚のことをカスゴ（春子）と呼びます。
漢字で「春子」と書くため春が旬と思われていますが、成長途上の魚ですから決まった旬というものはありません。ただし夏場より冬のカスゴの方が身に厚みがあり、味もしっかりしています。
『鮨 麻葉』の親方・塙直也さんが好んで使うのも冬のカスゴです。
「春のカスゴも使いますが、やはり寒い時期の方が身がふっくらしてるので握りに合います。とはいえ淡白な味の魚ですから、昆布じめにして昆布の旨みを入れ、甘みを引き出します」
塙さんが昆布じめに使うのは、5年間かけて熟成させたという真昆布。その上質な旨みを纏ったカスゴは小さなタイの幼魚とは思えないほど、ふくよかな味わいがします。

如月　第2貫

アジ　Aji (Horse Mackerel)

Winter "three-star aji" is just remarkable

Unlike other sliver-skinned fish like saba (mackerel) or sanma (Pacific saury), aji (horse mackerel) has a light, refreshing taste. Generally its season is early summer from May to July.
However, aji caught with pole and line in Izumi of Kagoshima Prefecture, famous for high quality brand aji, is more delicious in winter.
"Winter aji, especially the three-star aji, is just amazing. Those from Izumi are ranked between one-star to three-star. I always get the three-star. Yes, they're expensive but the quality of the fat is remarkable. Once you taste it, you will never want any others."
It is surprising how it melts in the mouth unlike ordinary aji. Slowly the sweet fat of the fish spreads as you chew and the flavor remains on the tongue.

冬の"3つ星アジ"は脂の質が違う

光りものの中でも清涼感のあるさっぱりした味が魅力とされるアジは、一般に5月から7月の初夏の頃が旬とされています。
ただし、ブランド産地として知られる鹿児島県出水（いずみ）の一本釣りのアジに関しては、冬が美味だと塙さんは言います。
「冬のアジ、特に3つ星のアジは絶品です。出水のアジは選別されて1つ星から3つ星までランクがあるんですが、僕は必ず3つ星を買います。高価ですけど脂の質が全然違う。一度これを知ったら、もう他のものは使えなくなりますね」
塙さんが絶賛する"3つ星アジ"を食べて驚くのは、アジとは思えないほどの口どけの良さ。噛むほどに甘い脂がじんわりと広がり、味の余韻が長く舌に残ります。

サクラマス
Sakuramasu (Cherry Salmon)

Early spring delight

Sakuramasu (cherry salmon) is a species of salmon. Like other Pacific salmon, they go down to the sea and travel around growing up, and then swim up the river to spawn. The name sakuramasu is said to have come from the cherry blossom season when they swim up the river. (Other theories exist as well.)
In the mainland of Japan, the best time to eat sakuramasu is early spring when they are loaded with fat ready for spawning. February is a little early but those who love the first of the season set great value and call them "hashiri" meaning "running ahead".
"This is sakuramasu caught in Aomori. It's hashiri but has good enough fat and the meat is soft. I cure just one side with cherry blossom leaf before making nigiri so that guests enjoy the arrival of spring."
A faint scent of cherry blossom leaf and the soft meat match perfectly, the taste of an early spring.

春を先取りした"走り"の美味

サクラマスはサケ目サケ科の魚。他のサケの仲間と同様、海に下り回遊しながら成長し、産卵のため川を遡上します。その遡上の時期が桜の開花の頃と重なるところから、サクラマスという名がついたと言われています（※諸説あり）。
本州のサクラマスの旬は遡上に備え身に栄養を貯えた初春。2月はまだ少し早いのですが、初物を好む人たちに"走り"と呼ばれ珍重されています。
「これは青森で獲れたサクラマスですが、走りとはいえ脂ののりは十分ですし、身もしっとりしています。季節の先取りということで、春が感じられるように、片面だけ桜の葉でしめてから握ります」
口の中でほのかに広がる桜の葉の香りと、サクラマスのふんわりした食感は相性ぴったり。まさにひと足早い春の味です。

Sushi Asaba, Nishiazabu

如月　第4貫

カキ　Kaki (Oyster)

クリーミーなカキに
煮ツメをつけて

Creamy oyster with nitsume sauce

There are varieties of kaki (oysters) such as Iwagaki oysters and Suminoe oysters, but magaki (Pacific oysters) is the most popular in Japan. They are farmed all over Japan and seen at the markets almost half a year from autumn to spring, but especially delicious in winter when the sea temperature is low.
"Winter kaki is creamy and goes very well with sushi rice. I serve kaki coated with nitsume (condensed sweet soy sauce) instead of anago (sea eel) when the quality of anago is relatively low from February to June. Kaki is wet when removed from the shell so I use dehydrating paper to get rid of water before making nigiri," explains the master.
The rich taste of creamy kaki and the irresistible flavor of nitsume fit together in perfect harmony and the flavor is enhanced so much you would want to dance. Aromatic zest of yuzu (Japanese citrus fruit) takes away the peculiar brininess of kaki completely.

カキにはイワガキ、スミノエガキなど様々な種類がありますが、日本人が最も多く食べているのはマガキ。日本全土で養殖され、秋から春にかけて半年近く流通しています。中でも際立って美味しいのは海水温が下がる冬です。
「冬のカキはクリーミーでシャリに合います。うちではアナゴの質が落ちる2月から6月頃にかけて、アナゴのかわりとして煮ツメをつけて出すのですが、殻から剥いたそのままだと水分が多いので、脱水シートでしっかり水気を取ってから握ります」
クリーミーなカキの濃密な味に、煮ツメのコクが加わった握りは、旨みの相乗効果で思わず小躍りしたくなるほどの美味しさ。ゆずの皮でほんの少し香りづけをすることで、カキ特有のクセも見事に消しています。

如月　第5貫

ムラサキウニ　Murasaki Uni (Purple Sea Urchin)

旨みのエキスが
舌を包み込む

Savory juice embraces your tongue

Uni (sea urchin) inhabit all seas around Japan. As harvesting season varies, they are one of sushi ingredients you can enjoy all year round.
The most delicious among those harvested near Japan are said to be kita-murasaki uni (northern sea urchin) and ezo-bafun uni (short-spined sea urchin) of Hokkaido whose wholesale prices are always very high at Toyosu market.
Even so, Mr. Hanawa says some uni from Aomori, Iwate, or Miyagi, are as good as high quality uni from Hokkaido.
"It varies depending on the season but uni from Tohoku (northern area of the mainland Japan), especially murasaki uni, is high level. This is murasaki uni from Ishinomaki in Miyagi but it's fresh and the taste is outstanding. So I serve in nigiri style instead of gunkan sushi for guests to enjoy the sweetness of uni directly."
When in mouth, the rough surface of uni instantly melts on the tongue as it transforms into savory juice like magic and embraces your tongue.

ウニもまた全国に分布し、産地によって漁期と旬が異なることから、季節を問わず楽しめる寿司だねのひとつ。
日本近海のウニの中で最も美味とされるのは北海道で獲れるキタムラサキウニとエゾバフンウニで、豊洲市場では常に高値で取り引きされています。
それでも塙さんは、青森や岩手、宮城のウニの中にも北海道の高級品と遜色のないものがあると言います。
「時期によって多少のバラつきはあるんですけど、東北のウニ、特にムラサキウニのレベルは高いですよ。これは宮城県石巻のムラサキウニですが、鮮度も味も申し分ない。だから軍艦巻にしないでそのまま握ります。ウニの甘さをストレートに味わってほしいので」
握りを口に入れると、しっかり粒の立ったウニが舌の体温で瞬時にして融け、まるでマジックのように旨みのエキスへと変わり、そのまま舌を包み込みます。

14　西麻布　『鮨 麻葉』

如月のマグロ（背の身）
February Tuna (Senomi)

Bring out the best taste by superchilling

Mr. Naoya Hanawa, the master of Sushi Asaba at Nishiazabu, chose this month hon-maguro (bluefin tuna) caught by set net in Himi, Toyama.

Pole-and-line, longline, purse seine are some of maguro fishing methods, but set net fishing is said to give least damage to the fish because the net is placed under the sea to wait for the fish instead of chasing it.

"Maguro caught by set net is delicious. They have rich taste and mild sourness compared to others. They are simply tasty. However, I have to be careful when aging because the color of the meat changes fast."

A block of vacuum-packed maguro is matured at superchilling temperature of 0 to 1°C, a method Mr. Hanawa found as a result of trial and error.

"I adjust the time of maturing depending on the size, part, and the method by which maguro was caught. This is a piece from the middle of the back so two weeks would be the best. The meat becomes soft with moisture and the flavor is enhanced by taking just enough time."

Nigiri sushi of this perfectly aged maguro is the best that you can taste with the sweetness of fatty toro (belly) and pleasant sour taste of akami (red meat) combined together. It matches very well with red vinegar sushi rice.

氷温熟成でピークの味を引き出す

西麻布『鮨 麻葉』の親方・塙直也さんが選んだ2月のマグロは、富山県氷見の定置網にかかったホンマグロです。

マグロ漁には一本釣り、延縄漁、巻網漁などの種類がありますが、定置網漁はマグロを追うのではなく、通り道に網を仕掛けて待つ漁法なので、最も魚体を傷つけにくいと言われています。

「定置網漁のマグロは味もいいんです。他の漁法のマグロよりコクや酸味がしっかり感じられて、シンプルに美味しい。ただし色変わりしやすいので、熟成のタイミングには気をつかいます」

塙さんは仕入れたマグロをブロックのまま真空パックにして、0℃〜1℃の氷温で寝かすという、試行錯誤の結果たどり着いた独自の方法で熟成させます。

「熟成期間はマグロの大きさや部位、漁法によって微妙に調整します。これは背の真ん中の身なので2週間ぐらいがベスト。じっくり寝かすことで身がしっとりとして、ぐっと旨みが出てきます」

完璧なタイミングで熟成させた背の身の握りは、脂の甘みと赤身の心地よい酸味が絶妙に混ざりあう極上の味わい。赤酢の効いたシャリとの相性も抜群です。

西麻布 『鮨 麻葉』

親方の塙直也さんは、日本橋や恵比寿、西麻布の店で修業し、イギリスの寿司屋でも働いたという経験の持ち主。
寿司だねの"熟成"にこだわりを持ち、その魚のコンディションや脂ののり具合によって微妙にタイミングを調整しながら、最大限の旨みを引き出す技術は、若手職人の中でもトップクラスと評されている。

住所：東京都港区西麻布 1-4-35 レ・フルール西麻布 102
電話：03-5786-6688
(ご予約電話の受付時間　13：00〜17：00
営業時間内は電話対応が
難しい場合もありますことをご了承ください)
営業時間：【昼】貸切のみ（完全予約制）
　　　　　【夜】18：00〜23：00（完全予約制）
定休日：不定休

Sushi Asaba, Nishiazabu

Mr. Naoya Hanawa, the master, trained at sushi restaurants in Nihombashi, Ebisu, Nishiazabu, and also has experience in England.
He specializes in maturing sushi ingredients. The master's technique to bring out the maximum flavor by adjusting the timing depending on the condition and the fat of the fish is at the top rank among young sushi artisans.

Address：1-4-35 #102, Nishiazabu, Minato-ku, Tokyo
Tel：03-5786-6688
Open：【lunch】By appointment only
　　　【dinner】18：00〜23：00（By appointment only）
Closed：irregularly

About Sushi in March
弥生 [3月] の寿司
寿司だねの特徴

長い冬が終わりを迎え、春の息吹が感じられる3月（弥生）。サバやヒラメなど冬の魚がピークを過ぎ、タイ（マダイ）やタチウオといった春の魚が登場してきます。
ただしこの時期に本当に美味しくなるのは魚よりも貝類。アサリやハマグリ、アオヤギ（バカ貝）など砂浜や干潟に生息する二枚貝の多くは早春に旬を迎えます。
もうひとつ、3月に登場する旬の味と言えば日本海で獲れるホタルイカ。中でも富山湾産の質が高いとされ、近年は軍艦巻のたねとしても使われています。

MARCH

Long winter is over and a hint of spring is in the air with the arrival of March, traditionally called "Yayoi". Peak season of winter fish such as saba (mackerel) or hirame (Japanese flatfish) ends while spring fish, madai (red sea bream) or tachiuo (largehead hairtail) for example, begin to appear.
However, the truly delicious is shellfish, because the best season for many of bivalves that inhabit sandy beaches or tidal zones, such as asari (Japanese littleneck clam), hamaguri (hard clam), or aoyagi (surf clam), is early spring.
Also hotaru-ika (firefly squid) caught in the Sea of Japan is the popular delight of the season appearing in March. Those of Toyama Bay are known for high quality and are used as ingredient for gunkan-maki (a type of sushi made by wrapping seaweed around sushi rice and placing ingredients on top).

Sushi Ichijo, Higashi-Nihombashi

弥生　第1貫

タイ Tai (Sea Bream)

Sakura-dai of the season is unbelievably sweet

Tai (sea bream), especially madai (red sea bream), is often said to be "the king of fish" in Japan and known as a precious fish eaten on special occasions. Especially in March right before cherry blossoms bloom, its value is at the highest and called by the special name "sakura-dai" (cherry blossom sea bream).
The master of Sushi Ichijo, Mr. Satoshi Ichijo, uses sakura-dai from Sajima in Kanagawa Prefecture famous for great quality tai.
"Akashi and Awaji Island in Hyogo are well-known but tai of Sajima isn't less of a quality at all. This one especially is very good. The sweetness of the meat is outstanding. As for tai, it is said what the fish eats decides the taste of the meat, so this one here must have fed on shrimps and crabs."
Thin layer of fat between the meat and skin is very delicious. So Mr. Ichijo does not take all the skin off when making nigiri.
When in the best season tai tastes so sweet you might not believe it's white-meat-fish, and you may enjoy the unique flavor similar to shrimps and crabs. This sensitive, complex flavor makes tai so special in March.

旬の桜鯛は、
白身とは思えないほどの甘さ

日本では"魚の王様"と称され、祝い事には欠かせない高級魚として知られるタイ（マダイ）。とりわけ3月、桜が開花する直前の頃のタイは"桜鯛"と呼ばれ、最上級の扱いを受けます。
『鮨 一條』の親方・一條聡さんが握るのは、上質なタイが揚がることで知られる神奈川県佐島産の"桜鯛"です。
「産地としては兵庫県の明石や淡路島が有名ですけど、佐島のタイもひけを取らないと思います。特にこのタイはいい。甘みが全然違います。タイは食べる餌が味を決めると言いますが、これは上質なエビやカニを食べて育ったんじゃないでしょうか」
タイは皮と身の間にある脂が美味とされています。なので一條さんは少しだけ皮を残して握ります。
旬を迎えたタイの身は白身とは思えないほど甘く、噛みしめるほどにエビやカニにも似た独特の旨みを感じます。この繊細にして複雑な味わいこそが、旬のタイの魅力なのです。

弥生　第2貫

シラウオ Shirauo (Icefish)

Steamed with sakura leaf

Shirauo (icefish) are little fish that belong to Salmoniformes Salangidae and live in brackish waters, where fresh water and seawater meet. Biologically they are close to ayu (sweetfish) or shishamo (smelt). The best season is winter but they are used as spring sushi ingredient in Edomaes because shirauo fishing at Sumida River was a spring event in the old days.
"Shirauo let us enjoy the season. I steam them with sakura leaves to add aroma for the guests to feel spring. To add more taste I put oboro (shrimp or fish flakes) in between and wrap with kanpyo (dried shavings of calabash, cooked and flavored)," says Mr. Ichijo.
Oboro add mild sweetness to the sakura scented Shirauo while kanpyo works as an accent to balance all perfectly. It tastes as fresh as spring and you may want to keep eating one after another.

桜の葉に包んで蒸し、
香りをつける

シラウオはサケ目シラウオ科に属する小さな魚。淡水と海水が混ざりあう汽水域に生息していて、分類上はアユやシシャモなどに近いとされています。本当の旬は冬ですが、かつて隅田川の白魚漁が江戸に春の訪れを告げる風物詩とされていたため、江戸前寿司では春の寿司だねとして使われます。
「シラウオは季節感を楽しむ魚。春を感じていただくために、桜の葉で蒸して香りをつけます。もともとの味が淡いので、シャリとの間におぼろを挟み、かんぴょうを帯にして握ります」
桜の香りを纏ったシラウオに、おぼろがほのかな甘みを加え、辛めに炊いたかんぴょうが味を引き締める、そのバランスは見事。後味もさっぱりとしていて、いくつでも食べたくなる美味しさです。

アオヤギ
Aoyagi (Surf Clam)

Enjoyable texture and aroma like flower

Aoyagi is shucked meat of shellfish called bakagai (surf clam). The name comes from Aoyagi in Ichihara City in Chiba Prefecture, where bakagai used to be gathered for shipping.
It is still one of Edomae sushi favorites although more and more sushi restaurants hesitate to serve aoyagi sushi because it is very difficult to cook them.
"Aoyagi doesn't go well with nigiri, raw or overcooked. Basically, I cook them with hot salt water, but must not bring to boil. I put my hand in the hot water to stir the clams, paying close attention to the temperature. When too hot, cool it down with some ice. This process is very difficult. When it is successfully completed, the clams become hornlike shape and taste sweet."
Aoyagi beautifully cooked with "horn" has just perfect firm texture. Fresh aroma like blooming flower spreads in the mouth and brings a smile on your face.

心地よい噛み応えと花のような香り

アオヤギ（青柳）はバカ貝という二枚貝のむき身のこと。その名前は、千葉県市原市の青柳という所がかつてバカ貝を出荷するための集積地だったことに由来しています。
江戸前寿司では定番のひとつですが、火の通し方が難しいため敬遠され、握る店は年々少なくなっています。
「アオヤギは生のままでも火を通しすぎても握りに合いません。単純に言えば塩水で茹でるんですが、沸騰させてはダメ。お湯に手を入れて貝を回しながら温度を計り、熱くなったら氷で冷ます。その加減が難しい。火の通しがうまくいくと貝がピンとツノを立てたようになり、甘みが出てきます」
見事にツノの立ったアオヤギはその心地よい噛み応えが魅力。そして噛んだ瞬間に花のように華やかな香りが口の中に広がり、心が浮き立つような気分になります。

Sushi Ichijo, Higashi-Nihombashi

弥生　第4貫

鼻腔をくすぐる潮の香り

ミル貝 Mirugai (Horse Clam)

Scent of crisp sea breeze tickles your nose

Mirugai (horse clam) is a species of bivalves similar to hamaguri (hard clam). The name came from sea staghorn, called "miru" in Japanese, often found on the siphon that sticks out of the shell.
They are not so well known but the market price is the highest among the bivalves. Sometimes the price per nigiri is even higher than otoro (fatty belly of tuna) because only the siphon is used for nigiri.
"True they are expensive, but I always get them when the good ones are out since they have everything I look for in shellfish, the taste, the scent, the crunchiness. Especially, those in spring have firm siphons and very delicious."
This day Mr. Ichijo chose mirugai from Okayama. The master dips the siphon in hot water to bring out sweetness before making into nigiri.
It's crunchy and crispy when you bite and at the same time fresh scent of the sea breeze tickles your nose while elegant sweetness spreads slowly on the tongue.

ミル貝はハマグリと同じ二枚貝の仲間。殻から出た水管にミル（海松）という海藻をつけていることがあるため、この名前がついたと言われています。
一般的な知名度は低いのですが、二枚貝の中では最も市場価格が高く、しかも水管の部分しか握りに使わないので、1カンあたりの原価が大トロを上回ることもあります。
「確かに高価ですが、味も香りも食感も貝の魅力がすべて揃っている寿司だねですから、いいものがあれば必ず仕入れます。特に春のミル貝は水管がしっかりしていて美味しいです」
一條さんが選んだミル貝は岡山県産。甘みを引き出すため、生のままではなく水管を湯にくぐらせてから握ります。
噛めばサクッと歯切れが良く、同時に爽やかな潮の香りが鼻腔をくすぐり、上品な甘みが舌に広がります。

弥生　第5貫

旨みを引き出す"漬け込み"の技

ハマグリ Hamaguri (Hard Clam)

Bringing out the best taste by "tsukekomi"

Hamaguri (hard clam) is a "kigo" (a word associated with a particular season in haiku) for spring. It is a sushi ingredient that represents spring in Edomae sushi as well.
Although it may vary depending on the origins, the spawning season is from April to summer, so the peak season of hamaguri is March right before the spawning season when they are fully nourished.
"They are soft, firm, and have strong taste in March. I use the 'tsukekomi' technique to make the best of this strong taste," says the master.
"Tsukekomi" is one of the traditional Edomae techniques. Mr. Ichijo dips hamaguri in hot water and then soaks them overnight in the condensed liquid made by boiling mixture of sugar, soy sauce, and sake. This extra work brings out more taste of hamaguri.
Tsukekomi hamaguri is so soft and the savory extract pours out as you chew.

春の季語にもなっているハマグリは、江戸前寿司の世界でも春を代表する寿司だねです。
産地による違いはありますが4月から夏にかけて産卵期を迎えるため、その直前にあたる3月は、身にたっぷりと栄養を貯えた旬のピークにあたります。
「3月のハマグリは身がふっくらしていて旨みが強い。この旨みを生かすために、うちでは"漬け込み"にします」
"漬け込み"とは江戸前寿司の伝統的な技法のひとつ。一條さんは軽く湯にくぐらせたハマグリを、砂糖、醤油、日本酒を煮詰めて作ったつゆ（調味液）に丸1日漬けます。このひと手間によって、ハマグリの旨みがさらに引き出されるのです。
漬け込みのハマグリの身は柔らかく、噛めば旨みたっぷりのつゆが口いっぱいに溢れます。

弥生のマグロ（蛇腹）
March Tuna (Jabara)

Sour sushi rice brings out the sweetness of the fat

"I'm not so concerned in the way how maguro (tuna) is caught nor aging them," says Mr. Satoshi Ichijo, the master of Sushi Ichijo at Higashi-Nihombashi. "Maguro that changed color by aging doesn't fascinate me. Appearance is also a part of the taste." Mr. Ichijo chose hon-maguro (bluefin tuna) from Shimoda in Shizuoka Prefecture, which weighs 71 kilograms. The size is a little small but it contains enough fat.
"The point is whether it matches our sushi rice. I choose one with soft meat and fine texture. I also look at the skin. If the blocks of maguro were the same size, the one with thinner skin tastes better."
He takes a piece of otoro with white lines of fat called "jabara" (snake's belly, from the way it looks) for nigiri. Sushi rice flavored with only red vinegar and salt without using any sugar brings out the sweetness of the fat to its fullest.

辛口のシャリで脂の甘みを引き出す

「マグロの漁法とか熟成についてはこだわりません」東日本橋『鮨 一條』の親方・一條聡さんはきっぱりとそう言います。
「熟成で色変わりしてしまったマグロには魅力を感じないんです。見た目も味のうちだと思ってますから」
そんな一條さんが選んだのは静岡県下田産、71キロのホンマグロ。魚体はやや小ぶりですが、しっかりと脂がのっています。
「基準はうちのシャリに合うかどうか。身が柔らかくて、肌理が細かいのを選びます。あとは皮の厚み。大きさが同じなら、皮が薄いマグロの方が味はいいです」
握るのは白い脂肪の筋が入った"蛇腹"と呼ばれる大トロ。その脂の甘みを、赤酢と塩のみで砂糖を使わない辛口のシャリが余すところなく引き出します。

Sushi Ichijo, Higashi-Nihombashi

東日本橋 『鮨 一條』

東京の下町・東日本橋で王道の江戸前寿司を握る店。親方の一條聡さんは日本橋人形町の老舗「六兵衛」で24年間も修業したという叩き上げで、江戸前寿司の伝統を受け継ぐ正統派の寿司職人。とりわけ酢じめや煮ものの技術の高さには定評がある。

住所：東京都中央区東日本橋3-1-3 奥田ビル 1F
電話：03-6661-1335
営業時間：【昼】 12：00〜14：00
　　　　　【夜】 17：30〜21：30
定休日：水曜日

Sushi Ichijo, Higashi-Nihombashi

An authentic Edomae sushi restaurant in downtown Tokyo, Higashi-nihombashi. The master, Mr. Satoshi Ichijo, worked at the classic Rokubei in Ningyo-cho, Nihonbashi for 24 years, an orthodox sushi master carrying on the tradition of Edomae sushi. Especially recognized for his excellent techniques of "sujime" (to treat ingredients with vinegar) and "nimono" (simmered ingredients).

Address：3-1-3, Higashi-Nihombashi, Chuo-ku, Tokyo　　Tel：03-6661-1335
Open：【lunch】 12：00〜14：00
　　　【dinner】 17：30〜21：30
Closed：Wednesdays

22　東日本橋 『鮨 一條』

江戸時代の俳人・山口素堂が「目には青葉 山ほととぎす 初鰹」と詠んでいるように、新緑が目に眩しいこの季節を代表する寿司だねと言えば、初ガツオです。
初ガツオとは春に黒潮にのって太平洋岸を北上するカツオのこと。秋の戻りガツオに比べて脂肪が少ないかわりに、酸味のあるさっぱりとした味わいがその魅力。
そして4月は3月に引き続き貝類が充実している時期です。愛知県三河湾産のトリ貝、そして北海道道東産の天然ホタテ貝などがピークを迎えます。
白身では冬のヒラメにかわってマコガレイやホシガレイが登場しますが、本当に美味しくなるのはもう少し先です。

About Sushi in April
卯月[4月]の寿司
寿司だねの特徴

APRIL

"Fresh green leaves, cuckoos singing in the mountain, and the first bonito of the season." This is a famous haiku poem composed by Sodo Yamaguchi, a haiku poet of the Edo period, describing how delightful it is to enjoy the seasonal things of early summer. The most popular sushi ingredient during this season when fresh green leaves shine in the sun is hatsu-gatsuo (first catch of bonitos in the season).
Hatsu-gatsuo moves up north along with the Kuroshio Current in the spring. It carries less fat than in autumn but the fresh and slightly sour flavor makes hatsu-gatsuo very special.
Also there are still plentiful shellfish this month as well, a wonderful season for torigai (Japanese cockle). Torigai of Mikawa Bay and natural hotate (scallops) of Eastern Hokkaido are at their best.
As for white fish, makogarei (marbled sole) and hoshigarei (spotted halibut) take over winter hirame (Japanese flatfish). However, it's not their best season yet.

Sushi Mana, Yushima

卯月　第1貫

カツオ
Katsuo（Bonito）

Enjoy the fresh and slightly sour taste of "the first"

There are various opinions as to when the best season is for katsuo (bonito). Autumn is said to be the best to eat as sashimi when they are fattest, but hatsu-gatsuo (first catch of bonitos) of the spring is highly valued for Edomae nigiri sushi.
"What makes hatsu-gatsuo so special is the profound and slightly sour taste of the red meat along with the fresh aroma. Autumn katsuo doesn't have all that. To bring out the best of hatsu-gatsuo, I take a block of katsuo and pass over the fire set by burning straw instead of using gas burner. It takes extra effort but grilling only the side with skin after applying small decorative cuts makes the skin crispy and the red flesh tasty."
Mr. Jun Kanai, the master of Sushi Mana at Yushima, does not use wasabi or shoga (ginger) but puts wagarashi (Japanese mustard) between the ingredient and sushi rice when making katsuo nigiri.
"This is a bottled wagarashi made in Kyoto, and it goes very well with katsuo. Every guest who has experienced this combination is surprised."
Not the unique pungency of wasabi but the mild accent of wagarashi lets you enjoy hatsu-gatsuo to its fullest without bothering the deep and sour flavor. The smoky aroma also creates a great harmony with hatsu-gatsuo.

初物の爽やかな酸味を楽しむ

カツオの旬については人によって意見が分かれるところ。刺身で食べる場合は脂がのった秋の方が旨いとされていますが、江戸前の握り寿司では春の初ガツオが珍重されます。
「初ガツオの魅力は赤身のコクと酸味、そして爽やかな香り。これは秋のカツオにはないものです。うちではそれを生かすために、ガスではなく藁の火で炙ります。手間はかかりますが、細かく包丁を入れてから皮側だけを焼くことで、皮はパリパリに仕上がりますし、赤身の味わいも引き立ちます」
そう語るのは湯島『鮨 真菜』の親方・金井淳さん。そして金井さんはワサビでもショウガでもなく"和ガラシ"をシャリとの間に入れてカツオを握ります。
「これは京都で作っている瓶詰の和ガラシですが、カツオとすごく合うんです。食べた方はみなさん驚かれます」
ワサビのツンとした辛さではなく、じんわりと辛さが伝わる和ガラシは、初ガツオの酸味やコクを邪魔することなく存分に味わわせてくれます。そして燻した藁の香りとも相性抜群です。

卯月 第2貫

アサリ Asari (Japanese Littleneck Clam)

旨みたっぷりのアサリを小丼で

アサリは日本人にとって最も親しみのある貝。北海道から九州の有明海まで広く分布し、炊き込みご飯、味噌汁、佃煮と様々な料理に用いられています。
江戸前寿司ではアサリもハマグリと同じように、甘辛く味つけしたつゆに漬ける"漬け込み"にするのが一般的です。
ただし金井さんは、砂糖を使わず、アサリの蒸し汁を醤油と味醂だけで調味したつゆに漬けます。
「旬のアサリは蒸すとすごくいいだしが出るので、その味を殺さないように甘さを抑えました。つゆを含んだまま食べていただきたいから、うちでは握りではなく小丼の形で出しています」
小さな身につゆをたっぷり含んだアサリは、噛んだ瞬間にだしの旨みが口いっぱいに広がり、その美味しさに思わず小丼をかきこむようにして食べてしまいます。

Juicy asari on rice in a little bowl

Asari (Japanese littleneck clam) is the most popular shellfish for the Japanese. They inhabit widely from Hokkaido all the way south to the Ariake Sea of Kyushu. There are various ways to enjoy asari, cook with rice, as an ingredient for miso soup, or simmer with soy sauce and sugar.
It is common in Edomae sushi to flavor asari by leaving in seasoned mixture, like hamaguri (hard clam).
However, Mr. Kanai does not use sugar for the mixture but adds only soy sauce and mirin (Japanese sweet sake) to the stock left from steaming asari.
"Steaming good asari makes excellent stock, so it shouldn't be made too sweet or otherwise kills the taste. I serve them in a small bowl with rice instead of nigiri style so that guests may enjoy asari with the broth."
Little asari soaked with special broth is entertaining from the second you bite and the taste so delicious that you would want to devour it.

卯月 第3貫

シロイカ Shiro-Ika (Swordtip Squid)

3日間寝かして甘さを引き出す

シロイカというのは俗称で正式な名前はケンサキイカ。しかもその地方によってマルイカ、ダルマイカなどと呼び名が変わります。主な漁場は山陰から九州北部。形はヤリイカに似ていますが、身に厚みがあって柔らかいのが特徴です。
「シロイカは身がしっとりして味も上品なので、握りにするにはぴったりのイカです。うちでは下処理をしてから氷詰めにして3日間寝かしてから使います。寝かすことでもっと食感が良くなり、甘みも出てきます」
しっかり寝かしたシロイカは、もっちりしているのに歯切れがよく、噛むほどに塩の効いたシャリとひとつになり、強い甘みが舌に伝わります。

Three days to bring out the sweetness

Shiro-ika (swordtip squid) is the popular name but the official name is kensaki-ika. There are various names depending on the region such as maru-ika or daruma-ika, for example. Mainly caught in Sanin and northern Kyushu area, it has the shape similar to yari-ika (spear squid) but the flesh is thicker and softer.
"Shiro-ika has moist flesh and elegant taste, so it is perfect for nigiri. Here I pack them in ice after cleaning and then let rest for three days. This process gives firm texture and brings out sweetness."
Well-rested shiro-ika is tender yet crisp. Furthermore, sour and salty sushi rice enhances the sweetness.

Sushi Mana, Yushima

卯月　第4貫

シロエビ　Shiro-Ebi (Broad Velvet Shrimp)

昆布じめで旨みを凝縮する

シロエビは体長わずか6センチほどの小さなエビ。富山湾の名産品として知られ、水揚げの直後は透明感のある美しいピンク色をしていることから「富山湾の宝石」とも呼ばれます。繊細な見た目とは違って旨みが強く、乾燥させたものはダシ材としても使われます。

金井さんはその旨みを生かすため、シロエビの殻を一尾一尾丁寧に剥いてから、昆布じめにします。

「シロエビは水分が多く、そのままでは握りに合わないので昆布じめにしてみたんですが、これが正解でした。昆布で挟むのではなく乗せる程度の浅い昆布じめですけど、それでも水分が抜けて旨みが凝縮されるんです」

昆布じめにしたシロエビを十尾ほど重ねた金井さんの握りは、まさに凝縮された旨みの塊。飲み込んだ後もずっと、旨みが舌の上に残っています。

Enhancing the flavor by the technique of kobujime

Shiro-ebi (broad velvet shrimp) is a kind of small-sized shrimp about 6 centimeters known as "the jewel of Toyama Bay" for the beautiful transparent pink color, mainly caught in Toyama Bay. Despite the delicate appearance, they have strong sweet taste so they are dried and used as an ingredient for soup stock.
To bring out the best flavor, Mr. Kanai uses the traditional technique of kobujime (curing with kelp) after carefully peeling each shrimp.
"Untreated shiro-ebi isn't good for nigiri because it contains much water in the flesh so I cured with kombu, which turned out great. Instead of putting the shrimps in between but placing on a sheet of kombu lightly cures and dehydrates them, enhancing the flavor."
Mr. Kanai takes about ten pieces of shiro-ebi treated with kobujime one over another when making nigiri. It is, to say, a chunk of savor. The exquisite taste remains on the tongue for a while after you swallow.

卯月　第5貫

トリ貝　Torigai (Japanese Cockle)

溢れ出る芳醇な海の香り

トリ貝も春には欠かせない寿司だね。例年3月くらいから市場に出始め、4月から5月にかけて旬を迎えます。北海道を除く本州全体で獲れますが、三河湾、伊勢湾、舞鶴湾のものが特に美味とされています。天然物はその年によって大きさや漁獲量に差があり、当たり外れがあるというのも特徴のひとつ。

「この三河湾のトリ貝はいいですね。身に厚みがあって香りも強いです。生のままでも十分美味しいんですが、クセを抜くために80℃くらいのお湯に数秒くぐらせてから握ります。それだけの手間で風味がぐっと良くなります」

鮮度のいいトリ貝は、お湯にくぐらせてもみずみずしい食感はそのまま。食べれば適度な弾力のある身から、潮風のように芳醇な香りと上品な甘みが溢れ出てきます。

Rich flavor of the sea pours out

Torigai (Japanese cockle) is also one of the most popular sushi ingredients of the spring. Every year they appear in the market from around March and the best season is from April to May. They are caught widely in Japan except Hokkaido but those of Mikawa Bay, Ise Bay, and Maizuru Bay are said to be especially delicious. One of the characteristics is that the size and the amount of catch vary each year as well as the quality.
"This torigai of Mikawa Bay is very good. The meat is thick and has strong aroma. It's delicious raw but I put it in hot water of about 80℃ for just a few seconds before making into nigiri sushi. This little process makes a drastic change of flavor."
Fresh torigai is still juicy and crunchy after dipping in hot water. You will enjoy the rich aroma like see breeze and elegant sweetness of the firm flesh.

卯月のマグロ（カマトロ）
April Tuna (Kama-toro)

Nigiri of the most precious otoro of kama-shita

Maguro (tuna) which Mr. Jun Kanai, the master of Sushi Mana, uses in April is otoro (extra-fatty part of bluefin tuna) of kama-shita called "kama-toro". Kama-shita is found below the gills of maguro. It is extremely rare for only a small amount can be cut from a big tuna.
"Kama-toro is deliciously fatty and the flavor is very impressive. So I use it whenever available. I'm not so obsessed with the aging but I put it in a box full of ice and let rest for four days to one week because kama-toro is fibrous."
Kama-toro has evenly spread fat like marbled beef so it melts fast. When in mouth, it only takes a couple of seconds for the sweet fat to cover your tongue. This leaves a huge impression.

稀少なカマ下の大トロを握る

『鮨 真菜』の親方・金井淳さんが握る4月のマグロは、宮城県塩竈産ホンマグロのカマ下の大トロ。通称"カマトロ"です。
カマ下とはマグロのエラの下あたりのこと。そのカマ下の身の中でも上質な脂がのる霜降りの部位をカマトロと呼びます。一本のマグロから僅かしか取れないという稀少品です。
「カマトロはたっぷり脂がのっていて、味も香りもインパクトが強いんです。だから手に入る時は必ず使います。僕はマグロの熟成にはそれほどこだわりませんが、カマトロには筋があるので、氷詰めにして4日から1週間程度寝かしています」
霜降りの牛肉のように全体に均一に脂があるカマトロは、融けるスピードが早いのが特徴。口に入れた数秒後には、甘い脂が舌を覆い尽くしてしまいます。それはまさに強烈なインパクトです。

Sushi Mana, Yushima

湯島 『鮨 真菜』

花街の風情が残る湯島天神下にひっそりと佇む、カウンター5席のみの小さな店だが、銀座の高級店にも負けない最高クラスの魚を揃えている。親方の金井淳さんは和食の修業経験もあり、握りだけではなく酒肴も絶品。日本酒の品揃えも豊富。

住所：東京都文京区湯島 3-46-6　TS 天神下ビル 1F
電話：03-6803-0190
営業時間：17：30～22：00
定休日：不定休

Sushi Mana, Yushima

Sushi Mana is located quietly at Yushima-Tenjinshita, an old Japanese geisha district. A small restaurant with only five counter seats but serves a collection of the best fish, even better than those you may see in Ginza. Jun Kanai, the master, has training experience in traditional Japanese cuisine and offers great side dishes not to mention nigiri sushi. Wide variety of Japanese sake is also available.

Address：TS Tenjinshita Building 1F, 3-46-6, Yushima, Bunkyo-ku, Tokyo
Tel：03-6803-0190
Open：17：30～22：00　　Closed：irregularly

About Sushi in May

皐月
[5月]
の寿司

寿司だねの特徴

春と夏の境界にあたる5月は、江戸前寿司のたねも春の魚と夏の魚が混在しています。
白身魚ではマコガレイに加えてホシガレイやスズキ（フッコ）、コチなどが登場し、貝類ではトリ貝、ホタテ貝と共にアワビが、イカはシロイカ（ケンサキイカ）と共にアオリイカが、寿司だねに加わるようになります。
そしてこの時期になると、産卵を終え黒潮に乗って北上を始めたホンマグロが太平洋側で獲れる回数が増えてきます。秋のマグロに比べて小ぶりなものが多いのですが、時にはたっぷり脂がのった200キロクラスの大物が揚がることもあります。

MAY

In May, both spring and summer fish are seen in Edomae sushi as the season changes from spring to summer.
White fish such as makogarei (marbled sole), hoshigarei (spotted halibut), suzuki (Japanese sea bass) and kochi (bartail flathead) arrive on the scene. Shellfish as torigai (Japanese cockle), hotate (scallop), and awabi (abalone), kinds of squid as shiro-ika (swordtip squid) and aori-ika (bigfin reef squid), join the line-up of sushi ingredients.
Also in this season there are more catches of hon-maguro (bluefin tuna) that moved up north with the Kuroshio Current after spawning. The size may be smaller than those in the autumn but big ones over 200 kilograms with a lot of fat can be caught.

Sushi YUU, Roppongi

皐月　第1貫

マコガレイ　Makogarei (Marbled Sole)

Thick ones are the good ones

Makogarei (marbled sole) is the most popular among more than forty kinds of flatfish, known as the typical white fish of spring to summertime while the peak season of hirame (Japanese flatfish) is late autumn to winter.
It inhabits widely from Hokkaido to Kyushu, and it is said that those caught in bay are more nourished and delicious than those from the open sea. The master of Sushi YUU at Roppongi, Mr. Jun Ozaki, says he selects makogarei by the "thickness".
"I look very closely when I buy makogarei at the market. Flatfish is literally flat but good ones are thick, especially at the back. These are not watery and have stronger taste."
Mr. Ozaki let makogarei stand for just one day before using for sushi. That is the best timing to bring out the taste yet leaving pleasant firmness. The more you chew the more taste comes out that you would not want to swallow.

魚体に厚みがあるものが旨い

マコガレイは日本近海に40種類ほどいるカレイ類の中で最もポピュラーなもの。晩秋から冬が旬のヒラメに対し、春から初夏を代表する白身として知られています。
北海道から九州まで広く分布し、一般的に外海よりも餌が豊富な内湾で獲れるものの方が美味とされています。
六本木『鮨 由う』の親方・尾崎淳さんは、マコガレイを選ぶポイントは"厚み"だと言います。
「マコガレイは市場で買う時にしっかり見て選びます。カレイは平たい形をしていますが、その中でも魚体に厚みがあって、背中のところが盛り上がってるものがいい。こういうマコガレイは水っぽくなくて、味がしっかりしています」
尾崎さんはマコガレイを1日だけ寝かしてから握ります。旨みを引き出し、なおかつ心地よい食感を残すためには、それがベストのタイミング。噛めば噛むほど旨みが出てくるので飲み込むのが惜しくなってしまいます。

皐月　第2貫

イサキ　Isaki (Grunt)

Strong taste matches red vinegar sushi rice

Isaki (grunt) is more popular in the Kanto region than in Kansai. Traditionally, grilled isaki was more commonly eaten than sashimi so it is said that it was after the period of high economic growth when the technology developed to keep fish fresh that they began using isaki in Edomae sushi.
Isaki has fairly large part of dark colored meat for white fish and a lot of fat even in early summer, so the taste is relatively strong.
"Isaki is firm so I let stand a little longer to make it softer to match the sushi rice. The fish has a lot of fat and strong taste for summer fish so it goes very well with our red vinegar sushi rice."
When you eat nigiri of isaki, you will enjoy the chemistry between the rich flavor of red vinegar sushi rice and the fat of isaki as sweet as that of blue-skinned fish. The flavor lasts for a while and the taste is still on the tongue after you swallow.

力強い味が
赤酢のシャリとよく合う

イサキは関西より関東で親しまれている魚です。かつては刺身より焼いて食べることが多かったため、江戸前寿司で使うようになったのは、鮮度のいいものが流通するようになった高度経済成長期以降と言われています。
白身魚としては血合いの部分が多く、初夏でもしっかり脂がのっているので、力強い味がするのが特徴です。
「イサキは身に弾力があるので、シャリに合う柔らかさにするため少し長めに寝かせます。夏の魚としては脂があって旨みも強いので、うちの赤酢のシャリとよく合うんです」
握りを食べれば、コクのある赤酢のシャリと、青魚にも似たイサキの脂は相性ぴったり。飲み込んだ後、旨みが長く残るのもイサキの特徴です。

30　六本木　『鮨 由う』

毛ガニ
Kegani (Horsehair Crab)

Crabmeat nigiri on seaweed

Kegani (horsehair crab) and zuwaigani (snow crab) are the two major delicious crab varieties in Japan. Kegani can be caught in the Sea of Japan but those from Hokkaido, the Sea of Okhotsk for example, are especially popular.

"This kegani is from Funkawan(Volcano Bay). Not yet in the best season but will be more and more delicious over the summer. We don't boil but steam to keep the savory flavor, and then carefully pick the meat for nigiri."

At Sushi YUU, the master does not serve kegani in ordinary gunkan-maki or temaki style but makes nigiri and place it on a small sheet of seaweed.

"This seaweed is called 'kontobi' and it smells great. It goes very well with kegani. The reason why I put nigiri on seaweed instead of rolling it around is because I want my guests to enjoy before the seaweed loses crispiness and gets soggy. I've tried many other ways but I believe this is the best."

Not only the meat of the legs and the body but also kanimiso (the liver) is added for the rich taste, which unites with the aroma of seaweed to be sublimated into indescribably mellow taste.

ほぐし身の握りを海苔に乗せて

毛ガニは冬のズワイガニと人気を二分する、日本の最も美味なるカニ。日本海沿岸でも獲れるのですが、特に人気が高いのはオホーツク海などの北海道産です。

「これは噴火湾で獲れた毛ガニ。今は走りというところですが、これから夏にかけてどんどん美味しくなります。うちでは旨みが逃げないように、茹でるのではなく蒸してから、丁寧に身をほぐして握りにします」

『鮨 由う』ではなんと、軍艦巻でも手巻きでもなく、握りを海苔の上に乗せて供します。

「これは"こんとび"という香りのいい海苔で、毛ガニとは相性がいいんです。握りを上に乗せるのは海苔がしける前に食べてほしいから。いろいろ試しましたが、この形がベストだと思います」

ほぐし身には脚や胴の身だけでなくカニミソも入っていて、濃厚な風味。それが海苔の香りとひとつになることで、えも言われぬ芳醇な味わいへと昇華します。

Sushi YUU, Roppongi

皐月　第4貫

アオリイカ Aori-Ika (Bigfin Reef Squid)

Bring out strong sweetness with moshio

Aori-ika (bigfin reef squid) is an essential sushi ingredient for summertime Edomae sushi. The body of aori-ika looks like harness called "aori" in Japanese and this is where the name came from. There is a high content of free amino acids, which the sweetness and flavor come from, compared to other edible squids, for which they are highly priced at the market.
"Fresh aori-ika tend to be hard but those we serve are so soft that guests ask if they are matured. It's not so. Applying slight cuts on the surface is the answer."
Not only the front side but also leaving sensitive cuts on the back is the special technique of Mr. Ozaki to make aori-ika so soft and creamy. Furthermore, it is the special style of Sushi-YUU to use salt called "moshio" made from seaweed to bring out the most of free amino acids of aori-ika. Anyone who has eaten the nigiri of aori-ika would be astonished by the unbelievable sweetness of squid.

藻塩をつけて
強い甘みを引き出す

アオリイカは江戸前寿司の夏を代表するイカ。その名前は胴の部分が障泥（あおり）と呼ばれる馬具に形が似ていることに由来しています。食用のイカの中でも甘みや旨みの元となる遊離アミノ酸が特に多く含まれているとされ、市場では高値で取り引きされる高級品です。
「鮮度のいいアオリイカは固いんですが、うちのは食感が柔らかいから、お客さまに『熟成させてるの？』とよく聞かれます。でもそうではなくて、包丁の入れ方を工夫しているんです」
表だけでなく裏にも細かく包丁を入れることで、柔らかく、舌にからみつくような食感に仕立てるのが尾崎さんの技。そして、藻塩という旨みのある塩を使うことでアオリイカの遊離アミノ酸の強い甘みを引き出すのが『鮨 由う』のスタイルです。
握りを食べれば「こんなに甘いイカがあったのか？」と、誰もが目をみはることでしょう。

皐月　第5貫

コハダ Kohada (Medium-Sized Konoshiro Gizzard Shad)

Master's technique to soften the skin

Kohada (medium-sized konoshiro gizzard shad) is not delicious at all uncured so it is the technique of Edomae sushi to make the fish "tasty" by sujime (curing with vinegar and salt). This is the reason why kohada is said to be the symbol of Edomae sushi.
Sujime of kohada is one of the most difficult techniques. It takes time and experience.
"Sujime of kohada is difficult. I change the amount of salt and vinegar depending on the size, the fat, and the season so I can't be more careful when I'm working on it. Kohada I have today has soft skin and nice fat so I'm trying to enhance the good qualities by curing."
Kohada has an impression of having hard skin but Mr. Ozaki's kohada is soft and harmonizes with sushi rice. When you eat, the sweetness of the fat dances on the tongue.

皮目を柔らかく仕上げる職人技

コハダは生のままでは美味しくない魚。それを酢じめを施すことによって"旨い"魚に変えるのが江戸前寿司の技です。だからコハダは江戸前寿司を象徴する魚と言われるのです。
コハダの酢じめは数ある技法の中で最も難しいもののひとつ。修得するためには時間と経験を必要とします。
「コハダの酢じめは難しいです。大きさや脂ののり具合、そして季節によって塩と酢の加減を調節するので気は抜けません。今日のコハダは皮目が柔らかく脂ののりもいいので、その良さが生きるように考えながらしめています」
コハダというと皮が固いイメージがありますが、尾崎さんのコハダはふわりとした食感でシャリとよく馴染みます。食べればほどよい酸味と脂の甘みが舌に心地よく感じられます。

皐月のマグロ（大トロ）
May Tuna (Otoro)

Fatty as autumn tuna

Maguro (tuna) Mr. Jun Ozaki selected this month was from Okinawa, big-sized hon-maguro (bluefin tuna) of 230 kilograms caught by longline fishing.
"Maguro in this season does not contain much fat despite the size but this one here is surprisingly fatty. It's rather unusual or I'd say I'm very lucky to get it." As Mr. Ozaki praises, the extra fatty otoro (the belly) is as good as maguro in autumn.
"Especially otoro of kama-shita (the rare part below the gills of tuna) has very high quality but sinewy so I cut the fibers before making nigiri. The lines melt by passing over fire so I also do 'aburi' (nigiri of lightly grilled fish) if requested."
Mr. Ozaki's maguro is cured until the meat is firm and soft, fresh and juicy. Sweet fat unlikely of maguro in early summer leaves you dreamy.

秋のマグロに負けない脂ののり

『鮨 由う』の親方・尾崎淳さんが選んだ 5 月のマグロは沖縄産。延縄漁で獲れた 230 キロという大型のホンマグロです。
「この時期は魚体は大きくても脂が抜けているマグロが多いんですが、これはびっくりするほど脂がのっています。珍しいというか、こんなマグロが買えて本当にラッキーです」
尾崎さんが絶賛するだけあって、大トロ部分の脂ののり具合は秋のマグロに匹敵するほど。
「特にカマ下の大トロの脂は質が高いです。ただし筋が多い部位なので、包丁を入れ筋を断ち切ってから握ります。筋は火で炙れば融けるので、ご希望があれば"炙り"もお出しします」
食感のことも考えて熟成させたという尾崎さんのマグロは、適度な噛み応えがあり、みずみずしくてジューシー。初夏のマグロとは思えない脂の甘さにうっとりとしてしまいます。

Sushi YUU, Roppongi

六本木 『鮨 由う』

2016年12月に開店し、たった1年でミシュランの1つ星を獲得。今や1ヶ月先まで予約が取れないという超人気店。客をとことん満足させようというエンターテインメント精神に溢れており、六本木の高級店としてはコスパの良さも魅力。

住所：東京都港区六本木 4-5-11　ランド六本木ビル B1F
電話：03-3404-1134
営業時間：【昼】12：00 〜 14：00（土曜日のみ）
　　　　　【夜】17：30 〜 23：00
定休日：日曜日・祝日を中心に月8日休み

Sushi YUU, Roppongi

Received one star in the Michelin Guide only one year after the restaurant opened in December of 2016. Now that it became one of the most popular sushi restaurants, you need to make reservation at least one month in advance. The master loves to entertain the guests and the price is reasonable for a high-class sushi restaurant in Roppongi.

Address：Land Roppongi building B1, 4-5-11, Roppongi, Minato-ku, Tokyo
Tel：03-3404-1134
Open：【lunch】12：00 〜 14：00（Saturdays Only）
　　　【dinner】17：30 〜 23：00
Closed：8days a month mainly on Sundays and National Holidays

水無月 [6月] の寿司
About Sushi in June
寿司だねの特徴

梅雨シーズンの6月は降雨量が多く、山のミネラルを含んだ川の水が海に流れ込むため、海水と淡水の混ざり合う汽水域に棲む魚介が身に栄養を貯えます。中でも江戸前のアナゴとシャコはこの時期に最も美味しくなると言われています。
寿司だねとしては数少ない淡水魚のアユも6月が旬。江戸前寿司では長時間酢につけて骨を柔らかくしてから握りにします。
そしてもうひとつ、コハダの幼魚であるシンコも例年6月末くらいから登場します。"江戸前寿司の夏の風物詩"と言われるほど人気が高く、シンコがたね箱を飾る8月下旬までの約2ヶ月間は、目当ての客が寿司屋に集います。

As the amount of rainfall increases in rainy June, rivers flow into the sea with rich minerals from the mountains, which let the fish living in the areas where fresh water meets seawater, store much nutrition. Especially Edomae anago (sea eel) and shako (a kind of mantis shrimp) are said to be the best around this season.
Also June is the season for ayu (sweetfish), a kind of freshwater fish, relatively rare as sushi ingredient. In Edomae style, ayu is soaked in vinegar for hours to soften the bones before making nigiri sushi.
Also shinko (baby kohada or baby konoshiro gizzard shad) appears around the end of June every year. So popular as to be called "the summer symbol of Edomae sushi", many shinko lovers rush to sushi restaurants for the two months until the end of August when shinko decorates tane-bako (wooden box where sushi ingredients are kept on the counter).

Sushi Hisaichi, Asakusa

アワビ
Awabi (Abalone)

Number one awabi from Boshu

Awabi (abalone) is one of the most valuable food sources you may see in the main dishes of Chinese or French cuisine not to mention Japanese. Those caught in Japan are especially known to be delicious and highly valued around the world.
Ise-Shima, Izu, and Wajima bordered by the Sea of Japan are known for great awabi but Boshu in Chiba Prefecture is said to be the best above all. The coast of Boso Peninsula is full of seaweed and this makes an ideal environment for the growth of high quality awabi.
Mr. Ichiro Deguchi, the master of Sushi Hisaichi in Asakusa, selected awabi from Boshu.
"From now to summer Boshu awabi is the best. We say 'they have heights' meaning the meat is firm and thick. These are very savory, and appetizing when simmered."
Mr. Deguchi uses special broth to make "niawabi" (simmered awabi) with pressure cooker and then uses for nigiri.
"Ever since I opened my restaurant, I have used the same broth to simmer awabi by adding little by little and taking special care of it. This broth brings out the deeper flavor of awabi."
Thick sliced awabi is soft but chewy, and savory juice floods in your mouth making you smile.

房州産のアワビは日本一

アワビは中華料理やフランス料理でもメインを飾る最高級の食材です。とりわけ日本で獲れるアワビは美味なことで知られ、海外でも高い評価を受けています。
産地としては伊勢志摩や伊豆、日本海の輪島などが有名ですが、中でも一番とされるのが房州（千葉県）産。房総半島の沿岸には餌になる海草が豊富で、それが上質なアワビを育むと言われています。
浅草『鮨 久いち』の親方・出口威知郎さんが選んだアワビも房州産です。
「これから夏にかけての房州のアワビは最高です。僕らは『高さがある』と言いますが、身がしっかりしていて厚みがあるんです。こういうアワビは旨みが強く、煮ると食欲をそそる香りがします」
出口さんは特別な煮汁を使い、圧力鍋で"煮アワビ"にしてから握ります。
「アワビの煮汁は開店以来、継ぎ足しながら使い続けてきたもの。これを使うことでさらに深い味わいに仕上がります」
厚めに切ったアワビは、柔らかい中に心地よい歯応えがあり、噛めば凝縮されたアワビの旨みが溢れ、自然と笑みがこぼれてしまいます。

水無月 第2貫

ホシガレイ　Hoshigarei (Spotted Halibut)

Feel the taste in the throat

Hoshigarei (spotted halibut) is a white meat fish that represents summer Edomae sushi. "Hoshi" means "star" in Japanese and the name of the fish comes from the round spots on dorsal and tail fin that look like stars. Hoshigarei is said to be the most delicious of all karei caught in Japan although surprisingly high priced at markets for the rarity.
"True, they are expensive but the taste is outstanding. So I buy whenever I find good ones at the market. Today I have hoshigarei from Miyagi Prefecture. The meat is thick and fatty."
Mr. Deguchi sprinkles a pinch of salt before making nigiri sushi to bring out more taste of the fish.
"The rich flavor is what makes hoshigarei so special. Just a little sprinkle of salt makes a huge difference."
You might think that the fish tastes a little simple the moment you put it in your mouth, but you will enjoy the rich taste of hoshigarei in the throat when you swallow and it lasts even after it's gone. This is the reason hoshigarei is so unique and popular.

喉の奥で感じる旨み

ホシガレイは江戸前寿司の夏を代表する白身魚。その名前は魚体の背びれや尾びれにある円形の斑点が"星"のように見えることに由来しています。日本で獲れるカレイ類の中で最も美味とされていますが、漁獲量が非常に少ないため、市場では驚くほどの高値で取引されています。
「確かに高価ですが、味は抜群ですから、市場にいいものがあれば買います。今日のは宮城県産のホシガレイ。肉厚で脂もしっかりのっています」
出口さんはホシガレイの旨みを引き出すために、握る前にほんの少しだけ振り塩をします。
「ホシガレイの魅力はふくよかな旨み。僅かな塩でそれがぐっと前に出てくるんです」
食べた瞬間こそ少し淡白に感じますが、飲み込む時に喉の奥で旨みを感じるのがホシガレイの特徴。そして飲み込んだ後も味の余韻が残ります。

水無月 第3貫

クルマエビ　Kurumaebi (Japanese Tiger Prawn)

Wild prawns of summer

Boiled kurumaebi (Japanese tiger prawn) is one of the classics you cannot leave out in Edomae sushi. Boiling is not only for preservation but also changes the color into beautiful red and increases sweetness by adding heat.
Farmed kurumaebi is good enough now that farming techniques have greatly advanced but "definitely non-farmed ones in summer," Mr. Deguchi says.
"I use farmed kurumaebi during other seasons but in summer it has to be the non-farmed. The beautiful color when boiled is totally different as well as the taste."
It is the unique style of Sushi Hisaichi to boil only for 40 seconds to bring out the full sweetness. Instantly the master removes the shell right in front of the guests and makes hot kurumaebi nigiri.
"Kurumaebi is best when eaten a little warmer than human temperature. So I make sure to serve at the best timing."

夏は天然物に限る

茹でたクルマエビは江戸前寿司には欠かせない定番のたね。茹でるのは保存のためだけでなく、加熱によって身が美しい赤色に変化し、甘みが強くなるからです。
育成の技術が進歩した今は養殖物でも味に遜色はないとされていますが、出口さんは「夏は天然に限る」と言います。
「季節によって養殖も使いますが、夏は天然物じゃないとダメです。味もそうですけど、茹でた時の色の鮮やかさが違うんです」
甘みを最大限に引き出すため、クルマエビを熱湯で40秒間だけボイルするのが『鮨 久いち』流。そして客の目の前で熱々の殻を剥き、茹でたての状態で握ります。
「クルマエビは人肌より少し温かいくらいが旨い。なのでベストのタイミングでお出しできるように心掛けています」

Sushi Hisaichi, Asakusa

水無月 第4貫

アナゴ
Anago (Sea Eel)

煮汁がアナゴの命

アナゴは江戸前の"煮る"技術を象徴する存在。関西以西ではアナゴは焼いて食べるのが一般的なのに対し、江戸前寿司では煮たアナゴにその煮汁から作る"煮ツメ"を塗るという独自のスタイルで供します。

それゆえに寿司職人が最も大切にしているのが"煮汁"。『鮨 久いち』ではアワビと同様にアナゴの煮汁も、開店以来12年間、注ぎ足しながら使い続けています。

「煮汁はアナゴの命。うちでは毎回使うたびに漉して、冷凍保存しています。少しでも品質が落ちたらそれで終わりですから」

出口さんは煮上げたアナゴをさらに網に乗せて炙り、熱々のままで握ります。食べれば芳ばしい香りが鼻腔をくすぐり、融けた脂と煮ツメの旨みが絶妙なハーモニーを奏でます。

Nijiru is the essence of anago

Anago (sea eel) represents the "simmering" technique of Edomae. In the areas west of Kansai, anago is usually grilled and it is the unique style of Edomae sushi to serve simmered anago brushed with "nitsume", thick sweet sauce made from the simmering broth.
This is why sushi chefs treasure "nijiru", the simmering broth. At Sushi Hisaichi, by adding new broth little by little, reuses the nijiru of anago for 12 years ever since the restaurant opened, like that of abalone.
"Nijiru is the essence of anago. We filter the broth after every use and keep it in the freezer. The quality must be stable."
Mr. Deguchi grills the simmered anago and makes nigiri while still hot. Sweet aroma tickles nasal senses, with the fantastic harmony of melting fat and sweet nitsume.

水無月 第5貫

アユ
Ayu (Sweetfish)

フルーツのように爽やかな味わい

川魚は鮮度を保つことが難しく、生食に向いていないため、江戸前寿司で使うことはほとんどありません。アユはその中の例外のひとつ。明治初期の寿司の絵に描かれていることから、江戸時代から使われていたと考えられています。

「今、アユの寿司を握る店は少ないと思いますが、伝統的な寿司だねですし、美味しいので是非食べていただきたいです。日本酒で割った酢に3日間漬け込むことで骨まで柔らかくしていますから、頭もそのまま食べられます」

出口さんが使うのは日本有数の清流として知られる島根県高津川で育ったアユ。それを地元の漁協から直送してもらっています。

「アユは鮮度が何より大事。それに高津川のアユは皮が柔らかく身がつまっているので、うちの寿司にはぴったりです」

清流で育ったアユは新鮮なフルーツのように爽やかな味わい。そして後に残るほのかな苦みが川魚らしさを感じさせます。

As fresh as fruits

River fish is difficult to keep fresh and not suitable for eating raw, so it is rarely seen in Edomae sushi. Ayu, however, is an exception. As drawn in some works of early Meiji era, it is said ayu has been used for sushi since the Edo period.
"Nowadays it may be difficult to find sushi restaurants that serve ayu nigiri, but it is one of the classic sushi ingredients so I'd strongly recommend the guests to taste it. It's delicious! You can eat the whole fish including the bones, even the head, because it is softened by soaking in the mixture of vinegar and sake for three days."
Mr. Deguchi uses ayu grown in the Takatsu River in Shimane Prefecture, famous for the clearness of water, directly sent from the local fishery.
"The most important is freshness. Ayu from the Takatsu River has firm flesh and soft skin so it is perfect for our sushi."
Ayu grew up in clear water tastes so pure like fresh fruit. And yet you can enjoy the slight bitterness of freshwater fish that follows.

水無月のマグロ（はがし）
June Tuna (Hagashi)

Otoro of "hagashi" so smooth and fluffy

The master of Sushi Hisaichi, Mr. Ichiro Deguchi, selected 120-kilogram hon-maguro (bluefin tuna) from Shiogama in Miyagi Prefecture, fairly fatty for June maguro.

Mr. Deguchi makes nigiri with "hagashi" of this maguro. Hagashi is made by carefully peeling off only the white tendons between the layers of meat to make it easier to eat. Usually sinewy part such as kama-shita (the rare part below the gills of tuna) or the back meat is served as hagashi, but Mr. Deguchi makes hagashi from a part of otoro (extra fatty part of belly) called "jabara" (translates to snake's stomach).

"When you use the finest maguro aged for a week, the tendons shouldn't bother in the mouth. Even so it makes a great difference when thin layers of tendon are removed carefully. You would feel the difference in the texture of the meat when on the tongue."

"Hagashi" meat is as soft and smooth as silk. You would be surprised how finest fat of maguro melts like powder snow.

"はがし"の大トロはふわふわの舌触り

『鮨 久いち』の親方・出口威知郎さんが選んだのは宮城県塩竈産、120キロのホンマグロ。6月のマグロとしてはしっかり脂がのっています。

出口さんはこのマグロを"はがし"にして握ります。はがしとはマグロの身から白い筋の部分だけを丁寧に剥がし、食べやすくしたもののこと。普通は筋が強く歯に当たりやすいカマ下や背の身を剥がすことが多いのですが、出口さんは"蛇腹"と呼ばれる大トロの部分をはがしにします。

「最高クラスのマグロですし、1週間熟成させているので、そのまま握っても筋が歯に当たるなんてことはないんですが、それでも丁寧に筋を剥がすと舌に乗せた時の感覚が全然違うんですよ」

筋を取り払った"はがし"の身は羽二重のようにふわふわ。食べれば上質な脂が舌の上で淡雪のように融け、思わず驚きの声を上げてしまいます。

Sushi Hisaichi, Asakusa

浅草 『鮨 久いち』

お洒落なカフェや飲食店が集まる話題のスポット"奥浅草"で極上の寿司を握る、知る人ぞ知る名店。親方の出口威知郎さんは銀座『久兵衛』で17年間も修業したという筋金入りの職人で、生まれも育ちも浅草という本物の江戸っ子。

住所：東京都台東区浅草 3-18-8
電話：03-3874-2921
営業時間：
【昼】
11：30（12：45 来店まで）～ 13：45（水・金・日曜日）
12：00（12：45 来店まで）～ 13：45（木・土曜日）
【夜】
17：30 ～ 23：00（火～土曜日）
17：30 ～ 22：30（日曜日・祭日）
定休日：月曜日

Sushi Hisaichi, Asakusa

A great sushi restaurant only real sushi lovers know serves the finest nigiri sushi in "Oku-Asakusa", a popular area in Tokyo, where fancy cafés and restaurants gather. Mr. Ichiro Deguchi, the master and a true artisan trained at the famous "Kyubei" in Ginza for 17 years, is a genuine "edokko" (Tokyoite) born and grew up in Asakusa.

Address：3-18-8, Asakusa, Taito-ku, Tokyo   Tel：03-3874-2921
Open：【lunch】11：30（12：45 last order）～ 13：45【Wed.,Fri.,Sun.】
　　　　　　 12：00（12：45 last order）～ 13：45【Thu.,Sat.】
　　　【dinner】17：30 ～ 23：00【Tue. ~ Sat.】
　　　　　　 17：30 ～ 22：30【Sun. & National Holidays】
Closed：Mondays

夏真っ盛りの7月は、海草を食べて育つウニとアワビが美味しい季節です。とりわけ、最高級のウニの産地として知られる北海道利尻島のエゾバフンウニ、キタムラサキウニの漁はこの時期がピークにあたります。そして光りものも美味。アジやイワシに加え、タチウオやトビウオにもほどよく脂がのっています。最近では、関西や四国で人気の高いイボダイを握りに使う江戸前寿司の店も増えてきました。
6月末から市場に登場しているシンコ（コハダの幼魚）は、成長してひと回り大きくなっていますが、柔らかい食感と爽やかな味わいはまだまだ楽しめます。

In July, the height of summer, sea urchins and abalones feeding on seaweeds are very delicious. Especially it is the peek harvesting season for ezo-bafun uni (short-spined sea urchin) and kita-murasaki uni (northern sea urchin) at Rishiri Island in Hokkaido famous for the best sea urchins.
Hikarimono (all kinds of shiny blue-backed fish) is also very delicious. Aji (horse mackerel), iwashi (sardine), tachiuo (largehead hairtail), and tobiuo (flying fish) carry good fat. These days more Edomae sushi restaurants use for nigiri ibodai (Japanese butterfish) popular in Kansai and Shikoku area.
Shinko (baby konoshiro gizzard shad), now grown larger, has been in the market since end of June but you may still enjoy the soft meat and the fresh taste.

Kamakura Izumi ginza, Ginza

文月　第1貫

アマダイ (アカアマダイ) Amadai (Tilefish)

Amadai from Wakasa Bay has exceptional scent and taste

Amadai (tilefish) is highly valued in the Kansai area. It is one of the precious and essential ingredients for kaiseki ryori (a traditional Japanese multi-course cuisine) in Kyoto and it is said most of the high quality amadai go to Kyoto.
For this reason they are not frequently seen in Edomae sushi restaurants, but the master of Kamakura Izumi ginza, Mr. Mikio Kamishiro, has a special connection for the purchase of the best amadai caught in Wakasa Bay of Fukui Prefecture.
"I think amadai from Wakasa Bay is exceptional in its taste and elegant scent. Especially the amazing scent is far beyond other white fish."
Mr. Kamishiro sprinkles salt and wraps the fish with kombu for six to seven hours before making nigiri to dehydrate extra water from the flesh.
"In doing so, the fish becomes sweeter and firm."
Amadai is known for the slightly sweet flavor as the name of the fish literally means "sweet sea bream". You would feel the sweetness the moment it is in the mouth and the taste becomes more profound as you chew.

若狭湾のアマダイは味も香りも別格

アマダイは関西で評価の高い魚です。京都の懐石料理には欠かせない高級食材であり、上質なアマダイのほとんどは京都に集まるとも言われています。
それゆえに江戸前寿司では握る店が少ないのですが、『鎌倉 いず美 ginza』の親方・神代三喜男さんは特別なルートで福井の若狭湾に揚がる最高クラスのアマダイを仕入れています。
「若狭湾のアマダイは味といい上品な香りといい別格だと思います。特に香りの良さは白身の中でも抜けてますね」
アマダイは身に水分が多い魚。そこで神代さんは軽く塩をあて、6～7時間昆布じめにしてから握ります。
「昆布じめをすることでより甘みを感じるようになりますし、身のねっとり感も出てきます」
アマダイの特徴はその名前の由来とも言われている、はんなりとした身の甘さ。口に入れた瞬間に甘みを感じ、噛むほどにそれが深い旨みへと変化していきます。

文月　第2貫

キンメダイ Kinmedai (Splendid Alfonsino)

Only the freshest become nigiri sushi

Kinmedai (splendid alfonsino) is found at a depth of a few hundred meters. In the old days, kinmedai was commonly simmered or dried because fresh kinmedai was not available. It has only been about twenty years since kinmedai became common in Edomae sushi.
"Kinmedai becomes fishy with time so I use only the freshest caught in Chiba. You can tell the fish is fresh by the firmness of the meat and the clearness of the eyes."
Mr. Kamishiro dips the fish, only the side with the skin, into boiled water and then leaves it in the special sauce for a while before making nigiri.
"I use only soy sauce, mirin (sweet cooking sake), and sake for the mixture. I don't use any kind of stock or broth that may ruin the pure taste of kinmedai. The purpose of dipping in boiled water is to soften the skin."
This specially prepared meat of kinmedai is soft and goes very well with the sushi rice. You would not feel any fishiness but be delighted by the sweetness of the fat that spreads on the tongue.

鮮度抜群のものだけを握る

キンメダイは水深数百メートルの深海に棲息する魚。かつては新鮮なものが流通していなかったため、刺身にすることはほとんどなく、煮つけや干物にして食べるのが一般的でした。江戸前寿司で使うようになったのは、ここ20年ほどの間だと言われています。
「水揚げしてから時間が経つとクセが出てしまうので、使うのは千葉で獲れた鮮度抜群のものだけです。新鮮なキンメダイは身に張りがあるし、目も透き通っているのですぐにわかります」
神代さんはキンメダイの皮目を湯引きにしてから、調味したタレに漬け込み、づけにして握ります。
「タレは醤油、味醂、日本酒だけで作ります。キンメダイそのものの味を生かしたいので出汁は入れません。湯引きをするのは皮が歯に当たらないようにするためです」
づけにしたキンメダイの身はしっとりしてシャリによく馴染みます。食べればクセは一切なく、ほどよくのった脂の甘みがゆっくり舌に広がります。

シンコ

Shinko (Baby Konoshiro Gizzard Shad)

Summer delight of Edomae sushi

Shinko is baby kohada (medium-sized konoshiro gizzard shad), the size of which is about a few centimeters. It is the popular summer fish cherished by Tokyoites who love the first catches of each season, and it appears at the end of June and plays the starring role until around the end of August every year.

"We use shinko for about a month until the end of July. Today I had to put four pieces for one nigiri because each was small but I'd say two bigger ones would be the best."

The preparation of shinko takes exactly the same steps as grown-up kohada. Each shinko of a few centimeters is trimmed with knife carefully, one by one, salted, and then vinegared. This process requires a very high level of technique.

"It takes so much effort to prepare many pieces but I can't skip every single process for the fans. Every year this season I get phone calls asking if shinko is in."

The taste of shinko is the same as kohada but the biggest difference is that it melts quickly leaving only the unforgettable savor and fresh scent.

江戸前寿司の夏の風物詩

シンコとは体長数センチのコハダの幼魚のこと。初物を好む江戸っ子がこよなく愛する寿司だねで"夏の風物詩"とも言われています。例年6月末頃から登場し、8月下旬くらいまでの約2ヶ月間は寿司屋の主役です。

「うちで使うのは出始めから7月末までの1ヶ月くらいです。今日のは四枚づけ（四尾で一貫分）のサイズですが、二枚くらいが一番旨いと思います」

シンコの仕込みの工程は親のコハダとまったく同じ。一尾一尾包丁で捌き、塩を振って、酢じめにします。それをわずか数センチの魚に施すわけですから、高い技術と集中力を必要とします。

「何十尾も仕込むのは大変ですが、お好きな方が多いので手は抜けません。毎年今の時期になると『シンコ入った？』というお客さまの確認の電話が必ずかかってきますから」

シンコの握りを食べると、味は確かにコハダなのに、数回噛んだだけですーっと融けてなくなり、心地よい旨みと爽やかな香りだけが後に残ります。その儚さもまた魅力なのです。

Kamakura Izumi ginza, Ginza

文月 第4貫

煮ダコ Nidako (Simmered Octopus)

信じられないほどの柔らかさ

タコには数多くの種類がありますが、寿司だねとして使うのはマダコとミズダコがほとんど。マダコの産地としては兵庫県の明石が有名で、夏に旬を迎えます。
「これも明石のタコです。大きさは2キロ。味も香りも他の産地とは違いますね」
回転寿司では茹でたタコを使うのが一般的ですが、江戸前寿司では"煮る"のが伝統の手法です。
「タコはしっかり洗ってぬめりを取ってから、醤油と日本酒、そして小豆を入れたつゆで煮ます。温度とタイミングが非常に重要なので、煮ている間は鍋から一瞬たりとも目が離せません」
神代さんの煮ダコは、それがタコだとは信じられないほどの柔らかさ。口に含んだだけでゼラチン質がとろけ、濃厚な旨みが一気に溢れて、あっという間に舌を包み込んでしまいます。

Unbelievably soft

There are various kinds of tako (octopus) but madako (common octopus) and mizudako (giant Pacific octopus) are usually used for sushi. As for madako, Akashi in Hyogo Prefecture is very famous and the best season is summer.
"This is madako from Akashi, which weighs 2 kilograms. Completely different taste and scent compared to those from any other areas."
Generally at kaiten-zushi (self service sushi restaurants where plates with sushi are placed on a rotating conveyer belt) boiled tako is used but in classic Edomae sushi it is simmered.
"Tako needs to be cleaned thoroughly to remove any residue and then simmered in the mixture of soy sauce, sake, and adzuki beans. The temperature and timing are very important so I pay closest attention and never leave the pan while simmering."
Mr. Kamishiro's nidako (simmered octopus) is unbelievably soft that it melts in the mouth. The rich flavor and aroma pours out to cover the tongue in an instant.

文月 第5貫

シロイカ Shiro-Ika (Swordtip Squid)

モンゴル産岩塩が
甘みを引き出す

シロイカとはヤリイカ科に属するイカの仲間。スルメイカやヤリイカよりも温暖な海域に棲息し、佐賀県呼子や山口県萩などが産地として知られています。
「シロイカの魅力は歯切れの良さとねっとりした舌触りを兼ね備えた食感、そして身の甘さです。僕はこのイカが好きで、夏場はよく握りに使います」
神代さんはシロイカの食感を生かし、なおかつ美しく仕上げるために、縦の包丁と斜めの引き包丁を組み合わせた技を使います。この細工によって、イカの表面が波しぶきのように立体的に浮かび上がるのです。
そして握りには煮切りのかわりにモンゴル産岩塩をつけて供します。岩塩の柔らかな味とシロイカの甘みは相性ぴったり。香りづけのすだちが爽やかな後味を引き立てます。

Mongolian rock salt brings out the sweetness

Shiro-ika (swordtip squid) is a kind of squid which belongs to the Loliginidae family, found in the warmer seas compared to surume-ika (Japanese flying squid) and yari-ika (spear squid). Yobuko in Saga Prefecture and Hagi in Yamaguchi Prefecture are famous for shiro-ika fishery.
"What I love about shiro-ika is the crispy yet creamy texture, and the sweetness of the flesh. I often use shiro-ika for nigiri sushi during the summer."
Mr. Kamishiro applies special techniques of decorative cuts vertically and diagonally on each slice for better texture and beautiful appearance. It makes the surface look like a wave in three dimensions.
Nigiri of shiro-ika is served with Mongolian rock salt instead of nikiri, sweet soy sauce. A sprinkle of rock salt enhances the sweetness of shiro-ika to the maximum while the aroma of sudachi, a kind of Japanese citrus, leaves fresh taste.

文月のマグロ（赤身づけ）
July Tuna (Akami)

Feel the luxurious texture on the tongue

All the restaurants introduced so far have selected toro (fatty belly of tuna) for maguro (tuna) of the month.
However, the master of Kamakura Izumi ginza, Mr. Mikio Kamishiro, has chosen marinated akami (the red meat of bluefin tuna).
"Akami is definitely the part you can enjoy the maximum sweetness of tuna. Especially in summer I'd strongly recommend akami. The purpose of marinating is to strengthen the taste and to bring out creamy smooth texture."
The amount of time for which tuna is marinated depends on the condition of the fish. When this timing is just right, you will enjoy glamorous creamy texture on the tongue. You cannot help but smile as you chew to feel the subtle sour taste of tuna and the rich savor.

舌に絡みつくような極上の食感

ここまで紹介したお店はすべて、その月のマグロとして"トロ"を選んでいました。
ところが『鎌倉 以ず美 ginza』の親方・神代三喜男さんが選んだ7月のマグロは赤身。それも"づけ"にしたホンマグロの赤身です。
「赤身こそマグロの最大限の旨みが感じられる部位。特に夏は赤身を食べていただきたいですね。づけにするのはその旨みを凝縮するため。そしてねっとりした食感に仕上げるためです」
魚体のコンディションによって時間を調整し、ベストのタイミングでづけにしたマグロは、舌に絡みつくような極上の食感。噛めば夏のマグロならではの酸味とコク深い旨みが力強く、味蕾に伝わってきます。

Kamakura Izumi ginza, Ginza

銀座
『鎌倉 以ず美 ginza』

ミシュラン1つ星の『鎌倉 以ず美』が満を持して銀座に出店。親方の神代三喜男さんは、目黒の名店『寿司 いずみ』で修業し、"いずみ"の名を受け継ぐことを許された唯一の職人。伝統を踏まえながらも独自の発想を加えた握りの味は、銀座でもトップクラス。

住所：東京都中央区銀座 4-12-1 銀座 12 ビル 8 階
電話：03-6874-8740
営業時間：18：00～22：00（閉店）
定休日：土曜日、日曜日、祝日

Kamakura Izumi ginza, Ginza

Kamakura Izumi of one Michelin star finally opened another restaurant in Ginza. The master, Mr. Mikio Kamishiro, had trained at Sushi Izumi, an excellent restaurant in Meguro, and the only master permitted to carry on the name "Izumi". His works of nigiri with tradition and originality is at the top level in Ginza.

Address：Ginza12 Building 8F, 4-12-1, Ginza, Chuo-ku, Tokyo
Tel：03-6874-8740
Open：18：00～22：00（close）
Closed：Saturdays, Sundays, National Holidays

葉月［8月］の寿司
About Sushi in August
寿司だねの特徴

8月はシマアジ、ヒラマサ、カンパチなど、亜熱帯や温帯の暖かい海に棲む魚が美味しくなる時期です。とりわけ産卵期を控えて身に栄養を貯えた天然物のシマアジの評価は高く、その味は夏の白身魚の最高峰とも言われます。

先月まで寿司屋の主役だったシンコは少しずつ姿を消し、それと入れ替わるようにスミイカの子供の"コイカ（新イカ）"が7月下旬あたりから登場します。こちらも新物を愛する江戸っ子に古くから愛されている寿司だねです。

そしてこの時期にはブランド産地"青森県大間"のマグロ漁が始まります。海水温が高いため脂ののりはまだまだですが、夏らしいさっぱりした味と爽やかな香りが楽しめます。

August is when fish that live in the warm seas of subtropical and temperate zones, such as shima-aji (striped jack), hiramasa (yellowtail amberjack), and kanpachi (greater amberjack), become very delicious. Especially non-farmed shima-aji is highly valued, storing rich nutrients before the spawning season, and it is often said to be the best of summer white fish.

Shinko (baby konoshiro gizzard shad), which had been in the spotlight until last month, is now gone while koika (baby Japanese spineless cuttlefish) appears in the scene, which has long been one of Tokyoites' favorite sushi ingredients for their love of "the first of the season".

Also in this season, maguro (tuna) fishing begins in Oma in Aomori Prefecture, an area so famous for maguro that it has become a well-known brand. Still maguro is not yet fatty enough due to high water temperature but you can enjoy light taste and fresh aroma.

Sushi Watanabe, Yotsuya-Arakicho

葉月　第1貫

イワシ
Iwashi (Sardine)

A little extra work for the best taste

Iwashi (sardine) used to be very low price, common fish in Japan. However, as the catch declined drastically in these 20 years, iwashi has now become one of the precious kinds.
Maiwashi (Japanese sardine) is good for sushi or sashimi. Those larger than 20cm are called oba (the big wing), 15~20cm chuba (the medium wing), and below that koba (the little wing).
"I usually use koba iwashi. They are not too fatty and the taste of the meat is stronger compared to oba, which is good for nigiri sushi. Today, we have so-called 'danjiri iwashi' from Kishiwada in Osaka. 'Danjiri' is the name of a huge festival held there every year. Also koba from Toyohama in Aichi Prefecture or Funabashi of Edomae are very delicious."
Iwashi has a little fishiness peculiar to blue-skinned fish so Mr. Watanabe sprinkles salt to dehydrate extra water out, rinses with sake and water, and then marinates in vinegar for just a short time.
"This preparation process makes a drastic difference. Iwashi is very soft and easily absorbs vinegar, so I have to pay closest attention when marinating."
When you eat nigiri of iwashi you would be surprised that fishiness has completely vanished and that you feel an elegant aroma. What is more, the fat is so tasty and rich that you might even mistake it for otoro (fatty belly) of maguro (tuna).
"Most people probably don't know iwashi can be this delicious. I strongly recommend summer koba iwashi even for those who are not a big fan of blue-skinned fish."

ひと手間で極上の味に

かつては非常に安価で、日本の食卓には欠かせない魚だったイワシ。それが20年ほど前から漁獲量が激減し、今では高級魚の仲間入りをしています。
寿司や刺身にして美味しいのはマイワシという種類。その中の体長20センチ以上のものを大羽、15～20センチのものを中羽、それ以下のものを小羽と呼びます。
「僕がよく使うのは小羽のイワシ。大羽に比べて脂がのり過ぎていないし、旨みが強いので握りに合います。今日のは大阪府岸和田の通称"だんじりイワシ"ですが、愛知の豊浜や江戸前船橋の小羽も美味しいです」
イワシには青魚特有のクセがあるため、渡邉さんは軽く塩をして水分を出し、水で割った日本酒で洗った後、ほんの短時間だけ酢でしめます。
「このひと手間をかけるかかけないかで、味は大きく変わります。ただしイワシは身が柔らかく酢が入りやすいので、酢じめには細心の注意が必要です」
握りを食べると青魚の匂いは一切なく、むしろ上品な香りがすることに驚きます。そして、マグロの大トロではないかと錯覚してしまうほどの上質な脂がのっています。
「イワシがこんなに旨い魚だということを多くの方は知らないのではないでしょうか。青魚が苦手という方も是非、夏の小羽イワシを食べていただきたいです」

葉月　第2貫

シマアジ　Shima-Aji (Striped Jack)

Unbelievably rich taste for white fish

Shima-aji (striped jack) is the king of summer white fish. A lot of fat but no fishiness, the elegant and light taste is very attractive. Especially wild-caught shima-aji is considered the most valuable in the market as well.
"Definitely non-farmed, without a doubt," says the master of Sushi Watanabe at Arakicho in Yotsuya, Mr. Masayasu Watanabe.
"There is a significant difference between natural and farmed shima-aji including their appearance. Wild shima-aji has beautiful stripes, sharp face, and wildness. On the other hand, farmed ones are dull."
Very fresh shima-aji has a firm texture so Mr. Watanabe ages the fish for 3-4 days.
"When serving as sashimi it is okay to be firm but for sushi they have to be aged. Aging makes the flesh tender to match sushi rice and brings out sweetness."
There are two stages when enjoying shima-aji nigiri. First comes the sweetness of the fat the moment it is in the mouth and then comes the rich flavor harmonizing with the rice. The taste is quite strong unlikely of white fish.

白身魚とは思えないほど
力強い味

シマアジは"江戸前寿司の夏"を代表する白身魚。脂がのっているのにクセがなく、上品でさらりとした味わいが魅力です。特に天然物のシマアジは市場でも最高級の扱いを受けます。
四谷荒木町『鮨わたなべ』の親方・渡邉匡康さんも「シマアジは天然物に限る」と断言します。
「天然物と養殖物は味も香りもまったく別物。見た目からして違います。天然は縞模様が美しく、顔つきもシャープで野性味がありますが、養殖は模様も顔もぼやけた感じです」
シマアジは新鮮なままだと身が固いため、渡邉さんは3日から4日くらい寝かしてから使います。
「お刺身なら固くてもいいんですが、寿司にするには柔らかさなければダメ。寝かすことで身がしっとりしてシャリに合うようになりますし、旨みも熟成されます」
シマアジの握りの旨さは二段階。口に入れた瞬間に脂の甘さを感じ、シャリと混ざりあった時に旨みがやってきます。その味わいは白身魚とは思えないほどの力強さです。

葉月　第3貫

キス　Kisu (Whiting)

Refreshing aroma like summer sea breeze

Kisu (whiting) is a general term for fish in the Sillaginidae family of the order Perciformes. There are several kinds caught in the coast of Japan such as hoshi-gisu (trumpeter whiting) or ao-gisu (small scale whiting) but when they say kisu in Edomae sushi it indicates shiro-gisu (Japanese whiting). Shiro-gisu is used in all kinds of Edomae cuisine including tempura, as there has been abundant catch in Tokyo Bay.
"Of course kisu from Tokyo Bay is delicious but I choose what is best each day regardless of where they're from. Today they are from Awaji Island in Hyogo Prefecture, very fresh."
However fresh the fish is, Mr. Watanabe follows the traditional Edomae sushi method of preparing it, gently pouring hot water on the skin of the fish and then letting it mature wrapped between sheets of kombu (kelp).
"I want to keep the meat soft so I mature it for only about an hour and half, kombu slightly touching the flesh. It is important to use kisu with firm body especially at the belly. They absorb more essence of kombu in the very short time."
You would be surprised at how soft the meat is when you eat nigiri with profound savor as you chew, fresh aroma of the sea breezes through the nose.

夏の魚らしい、爽やかな磯の香り

キスはスズキ目キス科の魚の総称。日本近海で獲れるものにはホシギス、アオギスなど数種類ありますが、江戸前寿司でキスと言えばシロギスのことを指します。東京湾でよく獲れることから江戸前の料理全般と関わりが深く、天ぷらのたねとしてもよく使われます。「東京湾のキスはもちろん旨いのですが、産地にこだわることなく、その日最も品質のいいものを選びます。今日のは兵庫県淡路島産で、鮮度もいいです」それが新鮮なキスであっても、渡邉さんは生のままでは使いません。江戸前寿司の古い仕事に従って、キスの皮目を湯霜にした後、昆布じめにしてから握ります。「身の柔らかさを残したいので、昆布じめと言ってもごく浅く、昆布を当てる程度でだいたい1時間半くらい。大事なのはお腹が固くて張りがあるキスを選んで使うこと。こういうキスは短時間でも昆布の旨みがしっかり入るんです」
握りを食べれば、ふっくらとした柔らかい食感に驚きます。噛めば深い旨みがあり、夏の魚らしい爽やかな磯の香りが鼻の奥に抜けていきます。

Sushi Watanabe, Yotsuya-Arakicho

葉月　第4貫

キジハタ　Kijihata (Red Spotted Grouper)

懐石料理のメインを張る高級魚

キジハタは瀬戸内海や日本海などで獲れる小型のハタ。関東ではあまり馴染みがありませんが、関西では評価が高く、京都や大阪では"アコウ"の名で呼ばれ「冬のフグ、夏のアコウ」として、高級魚のトラフグと同等の扱いを受けています。
「東京の寿司屋で扱う店は数少ないと思いますが、僕は京都で和食の修業をした経験から、キジハタの美味しさをよく知ってるので、握りにも刺身にも使っています」
ただし漁獲量が非常に少なく、上質なものは漁港から大阪や京都の料亭に直行してしまうため、東京の市場ではなかなか手に入らないのが悩みのたねです。「関西では夏の懐石料理のメインを張る魚ですから入手しにくいのは仕方ない。それでも少しでも多くの人にこの魚の魅力を知ってほしいと思ってます」
キジハタは味が舌に伝わるまで少し時間がかかります。口に入れた瞬間は淡白な白身という印象なのですが、しばらくするとじわじわと味が広がっていき、やがて旨みが舌を占領します。こんな白身魚はキジハタだけかもしれません。

Main fish of kaiseki cuisine

Kijihata (red spotted grouper) is a small-sized grouper caught in the Seto Inland Sea and the Sea of Japan, not very familiar in the Kanto area but valued in Kansai. In Kyoto and Osaka, kijihata has a different name "akou" and is equally valued as the precious torafugu (Japanese puffer), by saying "winter fugu, summer akou".
"There are only a few sushi restaurants in Tokyo that serve kijihata but I do both sashimi and nigiri since I know very well how delicious they are from training at traditional Japanese cuisine restaurant in Kyoto."
However, the catch is very small and those of high quality go directly to Kyoto or Osaka so they are rarely available at the markets in Tokyo.
"I know it's difficult to get them in Tokyo since they are heavily used in summer kaiseki course in Kansai but still I want more people to know how delicious the fish is."
It takes a little time for the tongue to taste the flavor of kijihata. The first impression when in the mouth may be simple and light but slowly the taste spreads and then rich flavor dominates the tongue. Only kijihata may have this special sensation among other white fish.

葉月　第5貫

ウニ四種盛り　Four Kinds of Uni (Sea Urchin)

全国選りすぐりの絶品ウニの饗宴

産地の異なる四種類のウニを小さな丼に盛りつける"四種盛り"は四谷荒木町『鮨わたなべ』の名物。全国のウニ漁の最盛期にあたる夏には、沢山のウニ好きが店に集います。「ウニといえば北海道というイメージが強いんですが、日本全国で獲れますし、産地によって味がまったく違うんです。関西や九州のウニも北海道に負けないぐらい旨いんだけど、東京では使う店が少ない。だったら僕が揃えられるだけ揃えてみようと」一念発起した渡邉さんは、休日を利用して地方の漁港に自ら出向き、東京の市場には入らない稀少なウニをいくつも直送してもらうことに成功します。「漁港から直接送ってもらうことで鮮度もいいですし、他の店では食べられないウニが揃っていると思います」この日は北海道礼文島のエゾバフンウニ、宮城県石巻産のムラサキウニ、兵庫県淡路島の赤ウニ、そして佐賀県唐津の赤ウニの四種類ですが、見事なくらいそれぞれの個性が違います。礼文島は甘みが強く、石巻はクリーミー。唐津は濃厚で味の余韻が長く、淡路島由良のウニは上品で、不思議なことにライムのような柑橘系の香りがします。

A selection of uni from around Japan

Sushi Watanabe at Arakicho, Yotsuya is known for serving four kinds of uni (sea urchin) from all different areas in a little rice bowl. In summer, when uni fishery is at its peak, many uni lovers gather here.
"You might think uni is mainly from Hokkaido but they are caught everywhere throughout Japan and the tastes differ depending on where they are from. Those from Kansai or Kyushu are as good as Hokkaido but rarely seen in sushi restaurants in Tokyo. So I wanted to collect as many kinds as I could."
Then the determined master visits fisheries far away from Tokyo on weekends and negotiates for precious uni, unavailable in Tokyo, to be sent directly to his restaurant.
"They are very fresh. Here I have kinds of uni you can not taste at other restaurants."
This day there were ezo-bafun uni (short-spined sea urchin) from Rebun Island in Hokkaido, murasaki uni (Japanese purple sea urchin) from Ishinomaki in Miyagi, aka uni (Japanese red sea urchin) from Awaji Island in Hyogo and Karatsu in Saga, each amazingly unique. The Rebun sweet, Ishinomaki creamy, Karatsu rich and long lasting taste, and Awaji elegant with aroma like lime.

葉月のマグロ（背トロ）
August Tuna (Setoro)

Sweet fat and rich meat at once

Mr. Masayasu Watanabe, the master of Sushi Watanabe at Arakicho in Yotsuya, has selected "setoro" from Funkawan (Volcano Bay), Hokkaido as the hon-maguro(bluefin tuna) of the month.
Setoro is chutoro (medium fatty tuna) located under the dorsal fin of maguro. It is the very precious part where you can taste both the sweetness of fat and the rich savor of red meat.
"Summer maguro is all about the aroma and the slightly sour taste. Red meat is okay just to enjoy sourness but setoro also has the aroma and sweetness of fat. I think this is the best."
Mr. Watanabe takes great effort to mature maguro as well. He wraps with layers of paper, puts in plastic bag, vacuums air, and then lets it rest in the refrigerator below zero degrees.
"Today this is matured only for four days because it was small but usually it takes about a week. The most important is the temperature and not letting the surface of the meat touch the air. That is where I pay the most attention every time."
Another point is that Mr. Watanabe makes thicker slices when making nigiri so that the guests enjoy the taste and aroma very well.
"Isn't it great to enjoy maguro full of mouth? When it melts on the tongue is the best moment of eating maguro."

脂の甘みと赤身のコクをいっぺんに味わう

四谷荒木町『鮨わたなべ』の親方、渡邉匡康さんが選んだ8月のマグロは、北海道噴火湾産ホンマグロの"背トロ"。
背トロとはマグロの背びれの下にある中トロのこと。赤身にまんべんなく脂がまわっているので、脂の甘みと赤身のコクをいっぺんに味わうことのできる極上の部位です。
「夏のマグロの特徴は酸味と香りですよね。酸味だけ味わうなら赤身でもいいんですが、そこに香りと脂の甘みが加わったのが"背トロ"です。僕はこれが一番旨いと思います」
渡邉さんはマグロの熟成にもこだわります。仕入れたマグロは紙で何重にも包んでからビニール袋に入れ、しっかり空気を抜いて、氷温に設定した冷蔵庫で寝かせます。
「今日のマグロは魚体が小さいので4日ですが、いつもは1週間ぐらい寝かせます。熟成で大事なのは温度管理と空気に触れさせないこと。そこには毎回気をつかいます」
味と香りがよくわかるようにマグロを厚めに切って握るのも渡邉さんのこだわりです。
「マグロは口いっぱいに頬張って食べた方がおいしいじゃないですか。それが舌の上で融けて、脂が溢れた時の快感こそが、マグロの醍醐味ですよね」

Sushi Watanabe, Yotsuya-Arakicho

四谷荒木町
『鮨わたなべ』

名店ひしめく寿司の激戦区、四谷荒木町でもトップクラスの人気店。京都の料亭での修業経験を持つ渡邉匡康さんの高い包丁の技術とセンス抜群の味つけ、そして地方の漁港まで直接足を運んで探した食材の質の高さは、他店の追随を許さない。

住所：東京都新宿区荒木町7 三番館1F
電話：03-5315-4238
営業時間：17：00～23：00（L.O. 22：00）
定休日：日曜日、祝日（加えて不定休あり）

Sushi Watanabe, Yotsuya-Arakicho

Top class popular sushi restaurant in Yotsuya, Arakicho, one of the very competitive areas for fine sushi restaurants. The master, Mr. Masayasu Watanabe, has training experience at a traditional Japanese restaurant in Kyoto. His exceptional knife technique, great sense, and the best quality ingredients the master looks for himself all around Japan go beyond other restaurants.

Address：Sanbankan 1F, 7,Arakicho, Shinjuku-ku, Tokyo
Tel：03-5315-4238
Open：17：00 ～ 23：00（L.O. 22：00）
Closed：Sundays, National Holidays, Irregular

About Sushi in September
長月 [9月] の寿司
寿司だねの特徴

9月を代表する寿司だねと言えば、イクラ。江戸前寿司では保存用の塩イクラ（塩漬けにしたイクラ）ではなく、新鮮な"生イクラ"を軍艦巻にして食べるのが一般的。8月から出回りますが、粒が大きくなる9月から10月にかけてが食べ頃です。もうひとつ、初秋にしか食べられない期間限定の味が"ソゲ"。重さ1キロ以下の成長途上のヒラメのことで、小さくても旨みは強く、心地よい歯応えが魅力。

まだまだ海水温が高いこの時期、日本近海のマグロの脂ののりは今ひとつ。そのかわり黒潮に乗って北上した"戻りガツオ"が旬を迎えます。とりわけ千葉勝浦の引き縄漁で獲れるカツオは、脂の甘みと赤身の酸味のバランスが素晴らしく、寿司職人たちの間でも高く評価されています。

September is the prime season for ikura (salmon roe). In Edomae sushi, fresh ikura is more common than ikura salted and cured for preservation. Fresh ikura appears in August but the best season is from September to October when the size of the egg grows larger. Another delight available only at the beginning of autumn is "soge", young hirame (Japanese flatfish) whose weight is below one kilogram. It may be small but has strong flavor and firm, chewy texture.

As for maguro (tuna), those caught in the seas around Japan still do not contain much fat due to yet higher water temperature. On the other hand, katsuo (bonito) moving up north with the Kuroshio Current is in the season. Especially, katsuo caught by trolling in Katsuura in Chiba Prefecture is highly valued among sushi chefs for the excellent balance between the sweetness of the fat and the sour taste of red meat.

Sushi RINDA, Meguro

長月　第1貫

熱湯にさらして食感を引き出す

イクラとはサケの筋子の膜を取り除き、ひと粒ずつをばらしたもの。大正時代にロシアから製法が伝えられ、日本に広まったと言われています。
筋子は加熱すると色が変化してしまうため、膜を取り除く時はぬるま湯を使うのが普通ですが、目黒『鮨りんだ』の親方・河野勇太さんは、まず75℃の熱湯にさらしてから、水洗いをします。
「熱湯を使うのは、その方が仕上がりの食感がよくなるからです。75℃というのがポイントで、この温度なら最初は熱で白っぽくなっても、しばらく置くと元通りの色に戻るし、味も変わりません」
丁寧にばらしてから特製のだしに2日間ほど漬け込んで味を含ませたイクラは、噛んだ瞬間にプチンと皮が弾け、極上のエキスが口の中いっぱいに溢れます。
「今の時期のイクラは、まるで卵の黄身のような濃厚な味わいがするので、それを生かすように心がけています」

Hot water makes them pop in your mouth

Ikura is salmon roe, taken out of membrane sac and separated. It is said the method originally came from Russia in the Taisho period and spread throughout Japan.
Warm water is generally used when removing the sac to prevent the roe from losing its bright red color due to the heat. However, the master of Sushi RINDA at Meguro, Mr. Yuta Kono, uses 75 ℃ hot water and then washes in cold water.
"I use hot water for better texture. The temperature of the water is the key, 75℃ is the temperature where the color may turn white at first but returns to its original beautiful color and the taste does not change either."
Carefully separated and marinated in special mixture for a couple of days, each ikura eggs pop the second they are in the mouth as savory essence pours out.
"Now is the season when ikura tastes so rich like egg yolk, so I try to bring out the best of it."

長月　第2貫

イカとウニ、
2つの甘さが融和する

イカウニとは河野さんがつけた呼称。山口県萩産のシロイカ（ケンサキイカ）の上に、北海道利尻島産のエゾバフンウニを乗せるという斬新な発想の握りです。
「イカとウニの味の相性がいいのはわかっていても、一緒に食べるとウニが先に融けて、イカの味だけが残ってしまう。そこでイカに細かく包丁を入れ、2つが口の中で混ざり合うようにと考えたのが、この握りです」
河野さんはシロイカをまず縦方向に細切りにし、さらに横からも包丁を入れることで、口の中ではらりとほどけ、ウニとひとつになるように工夫しています。
「切り方を間違えると握る時にイカが手に張りついてしまうので、イカの厚みによって包丁の入れ方を変えるのがポイントです」
握りを食べれば、イカとウニの異なる2つの甘さが融和して、まったく新しい味に感じるのが面白いところ。ゆっくり噛んでシャリと混ざると、さらに奥深い味に変化します。

Squid and sea urchin, harmony of sweetness

Ika-uni is the name created by Mr. Kono, an original nigiri sushi you must have never seen. Ezo-bafun uni (short-spined sea urchin) from Rishiri Island in Hokkaido is placed upon shiro-ika (swordtip squid).
"It is obvious that ika and uni makes a perfect match but uni melts faster and the taste of ika is left behind when eaten together. So I apply barely visible cuts on the squid for both to dissolve together in the mouth."
First, Mr. Kono leaves vertical cuts and then horizontal so the piece of ika breaks apart in the mouth and unites with uni.
"The point here is to change the directions of the cuts depending on the thickness of ika. Otherwise, it sticks to the hand when making nigiri."
It is very interesting how two different types of sweetness combine to become a completely new taste. When mixed with vinegared rice in the mouth the taste becomes more profound.

長月　第3貫

サンマ
Sanma (Pacific Saury)

Enjoy the change of taste each month

Sanma (Pacific saury) is a very popular fish, considered as the symbol of autumn in Japan, although it was not until 20 years ago that it joined sushi ingredients in Edomae sushi, when fresh and delicious sanma became available at fish markets transported by air.
"As for sanma, freshness is all that matters. Fresh sanma is nice and firm, which makes very good nigiri sushi, but can be fishy if not."
Mr. Kono applies grid pattern cuts before making nigiri so the contrast between the silver color of the skin and the red meat stands out.
"I do this style for now but when they become fattier I would lightly grill the skin and put a little liver on top to give some accent. Here I use sanma from August to October, and it is enjoyable how the taste changes with season."
In September the balance between the sweetness of the fat and rich flavor of the red meat is outstanding. The scent of scallion and garlic garnished aside stimulates appetite.

月ごとに変わる味わいを楽しむ

日本では秋の味覚の象徴として、万人に愛されているサンマ。ただし江戸前寿司のたねとして使われるようになったのは、刺身でも美味しい新鮮なサンマが空輸で運ばれ、市場に流通するようになった20年ほど前からと言われています。
「サンマは鮮度が命。新鮮なサンマは歯応えがありますし、身に締まりがあるので握りに合いますが、鮮度が落ちるとクセや匂いが出てしまいます」
河野さんはサンマの銀皮と身の赤い色のコントラストを生かすため、鹿の子（格子状）に包丁を入れてから握ります。
「今はこの形ですが、もっと脂がのってきて赤身がなくなってきたら、皮目を炙って肝を乗せてお出しします。うちでは8月から10月まで使いますが、時期によって味わいが変わっていくのも、サンマの魅力のひとつだと思います」
9月のサンマは脂の甘みと赤身のコクのバランスが抜群。添えられた薬味のネギとニンニクの香りが食欲をそそります。

Sushi RINDA, Meguro

タイのあん肝乗せ
Tai no Ankimo Nose (Sea Bream with Monkfish Liver Topping)

Amazing combination

Nigiri sushi of madai (red sea bream) served at Sushi RINDA is a little unique, with ankimo (monkfish liver) on top of the fish.
"We serve 'kawahagi (thread-sail filefish) with liver topping' for the limited season when kawahagi liver is delicious, and the idea came up to do this with madai."
Madai sent directly from the fishery at Uwajima in Ehime Prefecture, where the master is from, has soft meat and carries rich fat.
"Madai from Uwajima contains more fat compared to other areas of Shikoku such as Naruto because the current is milder. So, I decided to use ankimo to match with the elegant fat of madai."
Ankimo is steamed and made into smooth puree, and then ponzu (very popular sauce used in Japanese cuisine, made with soy sauce, citrus extract, vinegar, etc.) and scallions are added. This process is necessary so the strong fat of ankimo does not bother the delicate flavor of the madai beneath.
"Some people may not imagine eating them together but I'm sure they would be surprised at the great harmony."

驚きの相性の良さ

目黒『鮨 りんだ』のタイ（マダイ）の握りは少し変わっています。タイの切り身の上に、あん肝が乗っているのです。
「カワハギの肝の美味しい時期に"カワハギの身の肝乗せ"をお出ししているんですが、ふと、これをタイでやったらどうだろう？と思いついたんです」
親方の地元である愛媛県宇和島の漁師さんから直送してもらったタイは、身がふっくらして脂もしっかりのっています。
「宇和島のタイは同じ四国でも鳴門のタイとは違って、潮の流れがゆるやかな場所を泳いでいるので脂があるんです。その上品な脂と合わせるために、あん肝を使うことにしました」
あん肝とはアンコウという魚の肝臓。脂が強いので、蒸して裏ごしした後、ポン酢と白ネギを加えて、タイの繊細な味わいを壊さないように工夫しています。
「ミスマッチと感じる方もいると思いますが、食べていただければ、2つの相性の良さに驚かれるのではないでしょうか」

カマス Kamasu (Barracuda)

Tasty fat overflowing from under crispy skin

Kamasu (barracuda) is a fish of the family Sphyraena in the order Perciformes. Due to its high water content in the flesh, it is generally dried and grilled instead of eaten as sashimi or nigiri sushi.
"Kamasu is a very tasty fish but only the fatty ones are suitable for nigiri. So kamasu that can be used for sushi is limited. Recent fishermen have profound knowledge so when they catch kamasu with rich fat they are sorted out and shipped separately after being soaked in salt water. These specially selected kamasu end up with unbelievable price."
Mr. Kono sprinkles salt to draw more water out from the meat, brushes soy sauce on the skin, lightly seared, and then finally makes nigiri. Smoky aroma of soy sauce arouses appetite and tasty fat overflows from under the crispy skin.

パリパリの皮の下から脂が溢れる

カマスはスズキ目カマス科に属する魚。身に水分が多く脂肪が少ないのが特徴で、刺身や握り寿司にすることはほとんどなく、干物にして焼いて食べるのが一般的です。
「カマスは美味しい魚ですが、脂がのっていないと握りには合いません。なので寿司に使えるカマスは限られています。最近の漁師さんは知識があるので、脂ののったカマスが獲れた時はたて塩（濃い塩水）につけてしめて、選別して出荷するんです。そのかわり驚くような高い値段がついていたりします」
河野さんはそのカマスにさらにひと塩して水分を抜き、皮目に醤油を塗り、炙って焼き色をつけてから握りにします。
炙った醤油の芳ばしい香りが食欲をそそり、食べれば、パリパリの皮の下から旨みたっぷりの脂が溢れます。

長月のマグロ（大西洋マグロのはがし）
September Tuna (Hagashi of Atlantic Bluefin Tuna)

Enjoying the smooth and elegant fat

This month Mr. Kono, the master of Sushi RINDA at Meguro, uses Atlantic bluefin tuna caught in Boston, U.S.A.

"I used to work at a sushi restaurant in New York for three years, and there I used Atlantic bluefin tuna. So it's special for me. The quality is as good as those in Japan and it has fine, smooth fat although the body may be larger. The tendon is a little bothering so I slice all pieces of tendon and sinew off of the otoro area."

Mr. Kono performs a technique called "hagashi" to remove the white tendon. He uses the knife along, not against, the tendon and very carefully removes each of them. Only the truly skilled sushi chefs can do this.

"Boston maguro is firmer so I use a couple pieces of thin sliced meat to make nigiri. This makes more surface to touch the tongue for the fat to melt faster."

Four layers of sliced otoro are so soft and smooth you don't even have to chew. The fat melts in a second, leaving only the supreme aroma.

さらりとして品のいい脂を楽しむ

目黒『鮨 りんだ』の親方・河野勇太さんが握る9月のマグロは、アメリカ、ボストンで獲れた大西洋マグロです。

大西洋マグロはかつては日本近海のホンマグロと同じ種類と考えられていましたが、エラの数や筋肉のつき方が異なることから、亜種または別種と考えられています。

「僕はニューヨークの寿司屋に3年間いて、大西洋マグロを使っていたので愛着があるんです。味は国産のホンマグロと遜色ないですし、魚体は大きくても脂はさらりとして品がいい。ただし筋が太くて歯に当たるので、大トロの部分は包丁で筋を外します」

河野さんは"はがし"と呼ばれる手法でマグロの白い筋を外します。筋に逆らうのではなく沿うようにして包丁を入れ、丁寧に切り取っていきます。これは高い技術を持つ寿司職人にしかできません。

「ボストンの大西洋マグロは少し身が固いので、筋を外した身を薄切りにして、数枚重ねてから握ります。こうすると舌に触れる面積が増えて、脂が融けやすくなるんです」

薄切りを四枚重ねにした大トロは、噛む必要がないほどの柔らかさ。舌に乗せればあっという間に甘い脂が融け、口いっぱいに広がります。

Sushi RINDA, Meguro

目黒『鮨 りんだ』

伝統的な技法を踏まえつつ、そこに斬新な発想を加えた、江戸前寿司のニューウェーブを代表する店。親方の河野勇太さんは30代の若手ながら、包丁の技術が高く、ニューヨークの寿司屋で3年間握ったという経験を持つ。

住所：東京都目黒区下目黒 2-24-12 イメージスタジオ 109 1F
電話：03-6420-3343
営業時間：18:00～23:00
定休日：日曜日、月曜日

Sushi RINDA, Meguro

One of the new wave of sushi restaurants with tradition and creativity. Mr. Yuta Kono, the young master in his thirties, has great technique with knifes and has three years of experience in New York.

Address：Image Studio 109 1F, 2-24-12, Shimomeguro, Meguro-ku, Tokyo
Tel：03-6420-3343
Open：18:00～23:00
Closed：Sundays and Mondays

About Sushi in October

長月
[10月]
の寿司

寿司だねの特徴

秋本番の10月。海水温も下がり、夏の魚と秋の魚がすっかり入れ替わります。白身ではシマアジにかわってアマダイに脂がのり、光り物ではアジやイワシのかわりにサバやカマスが美味しくなってきます。シンコやコイカは成長し、大人のコハダ、スミイカへと変わります。そしていよいよ、青森県大間や三廐など津軽海峡で獲れるマグロが本格的なシーズンに入ります。さっぱりした味の夏のマグロに対し、脂肪をつけた秋のマグロは旨みもぐっと濃厚になります。
もうひとつ、この時期にしか食べられない季節限定の味が"天上ブリ"。北海道の積丹半島沖まで北上したブリを定置網で捕えたもので、真冬に獲れる寒ブリに比べて脂ののりがほどよく、上品な味わいが特徴です。

OCTOBER

This month, in the midst of the fall, sea temperature declines and the autumn fish completely takes over summer fish. As for white fish, amadai (tilefish) becomes nice and fatty to take the place of shima-aji (striped jack) while saba (mackerel) and kamasu (barracuda) become more delicious than aji (horse mackerel) and iwashi (sardine). Shinko (baby kohada) grows up to be kohada (medium-sized konoshiro gizzard shad) and koika (baby sumi-ika) to be sumi-ika (Japanese spineless cuttlefish).
Finally, the season for maguro (tuna) arrives in Oma and Minmaya in Aomori Prefecture. Summer maguro has light taste while autumn maguro contains much fat with richer taste. Another precious fish that can only be eaten this season is the "tenjo-buri" meaning "yellowtail from heaven", special buri that swims up north as far as the Shakotan Peninsula in Hokkaido caught by set net. Tenjo-buri carries less fat compared to kan-buri (winter yellowtail) and the taste is more elegant.

Sushi Suzuki, Ginza

ブリ
Buri (Yellowtail)

The sweet experience only for this season

Buri (yellowtail) has different names for each stage of growth so it is called "shusse-uo", which means "fish that climb up the ladder". Those about 20cm are called "wakashi", 40cm "inada", 60cm "warasa", and especially bigger ones above one meter are called "buri" at fish markets in Tokyo.
Fully-grown buri swims up north along the coast of Japan from spring to summer and reaches Hokkaido in September to October. Only those caught by set net off the coast of the Shakotan Peninsula may be called the "tenjo-buri", a very popular sushi ingredient. The master of Sushi Suzuki at Ginza, Mr. Takahisa Suzuki, likes to include this tenjo-buri in his course of sushi.
"Autumn buri is very delicious in the way different from winter buri. Carries moderate fat and it's sweet, so goes very well with our sushi rice. I slice them thin for nigiri because the meat is a little firm."
Three thin slices from the belly of buri, one over another, make one piece of nigiri sushi. It is soft but also nicely firm, and the sour rice enhances the sweetness of the fat.

この季節にしか味わえない脂の甘さ

ブリは成長段階に応じて呼称が変わる"出世魚"。東京の市場では体長20センチ前後のものを『ワカシ』、40センチ前後を『イナダ』、60センチ前後を『ワラサ』、そして1メートル以上に達した大型のものを『ブリ』と呼びます。
成長したブリは春から夏にかけ日本近海を北上し、9月から10月にかけて北海道に到達します。このうち積丹半島沖の定置網で獲れたものを"天上ブリ"と呼び、人気の寿司だねとなっています。
銀座『鮨 鈴木』の親方・鈴木孝尚さんも、この天上ブリを好んで使います。
「この時期のブリは、真冬の寒ブリとは違う美味しさ。ほどよく脂がのっていて、その脂が甘いんですよね。だからうちのシャリと相性がいいんです。ただし身が少し固いので、薄く切りつけてから握ります」
紙のように薄く切ったブリの腹の身を三枚重ねにした握りは、ふわりとした食感ながら適度な歯応えがあり、噛めば辛口のシャリと渾然一体となって、脂の甘さがさらに際立ちます。

神無月 第2貫

シラカワ Shirakawa (White Tilefish)

Almost extinct tilefish that shines silvery white

Although commonly called shirakawa, the official name is shiro-amadai (white tilefish). It is said to be the most delicious among all kinds of amadai (tilefish) found in the seas around Japan, shining mysteriously silvery white, very rarely seen at any market. It is known as the most precious amadai and sold at surprisingly high price, even over 100,000 yen for just one shirakawa.
"I just adore shirakawa. It is perfect grilled, steamed, or as fresh sashimi. Best white fish for sushi. So I purchase it no matter how high the price."
Mr. Suzuki says the texture of the meat is completely different between shirakawa and aka-amadai (red tilefish) even though they both belong to the same category of amadai.
"Aka-amadai needs to be cured with kombu to take out extra moisture out of the meat but this process is not necessary for shirakawa, and the taste is enhanced by itself with time. So the guests ask me if I have done anything to the fish when the fish is served raw without being cured at all."
Shirakawa is very unique to enjoy. Usually, you would feel the sweetness of the fat and then the taste of the meat but as for shirakawa both at once. It is so rich and long lasting you would want to ask for good Japanese sake to go with the nigiri.

銀白色に輝く幻のアマダイ

シラカワというのは俗称で、正式な名前はシロアマダイ。日本近海に棲むアマダイの仲間では最も美味とされ、銀白色に輝く神秘的な魚体を持ち、漁獲量が極めて少ないことから"幻のアマダイ"と呼ばれています。ゆえに市場では驚くほど高価で取り引きされ、一尾10万円以上の値がつくことも。
「シラカワは大好きな魚。刺身だけじゃなくて、焼いても蒸しても旨い万能の魚ですよね。寿司だねとしても白身魚の中の最上級。だから『えっ？』という高値でも、思いきって買います」
鈴木さんは、同じアマダイでもシラカワとアカアマダイでは身の質がまったく違うと言います。
「アカアマダイは水分が多い魚なので昆布じめにしたりするんですが、シラカワはその必要がない。しかも寝かすことでどんどん旨みが出てくる。だから生で出しても、お客さんに『これ、昆布じめしてるの？』と聞かれたりします」
シラカワは味わいも独特、普通の白身魚であればまず脂の甘みを感じ、それからじわじわと旨みが伝わるのですが、シラカワは甘みと旨みがいっぺんにやってきます。その旨みはふくよかで余韻が長いので、日本酒と合わせるとさらに美味しくなります。

神無月 第3貫

ハマグリ Hamaguri (Hard Clam)

The overflowing savor

Hamaguri (hard clam) is one of the classics of Edomae sushi. Unlike akagai (ark shell), hamaguri is not served raw but lightly boiled and flavored with special sauce. The sauce is made with broth from boiling hamaguri.
"Here I add Japanese sake, soy sauce and crystallized brown sugar to the broth and simmer until very thick. The purpose is to condense the rich flavor of hamaguri that poured out by boiling and returning it back again."
Carefully undercooked hamaguri is very soft and amazingly juicy. It is the traditional Edomae style to brush on sauce called "nitsume" made with broth from simmering anago (sea eel).
The essence of hamaguri overflows and as the two different tastes of hamaguri and anago combine, it feels as if the flavor expands in the mouth.

噛めば旨みエキスが溢れる

ハマグリは古くから江戸前寿司の定番のたね。ただし赤貝のように生のままで出すわけではなく、軽く下茹でにしてから、茹で汁を煮詰めたタレに漬け込んだものを握ります。
「うちでは茹で汁に日本酒、醤油、ザラメを加えてさらに煮詰めて、アメのような状態にしてから漬け込みます。茹で汁に溶け出た旨みを凝縮して、もう一度ハマグリに戻すというイメージですね」
火の通しが浅いので、ハマグリの身は柔らかく、驚くほどジューシー。そして、その上からアナゴの煮汁で作った煮ツメをかけるのが伝統的な江戸前の作法。
握りを食べればハマグリの旨みエキスが溢れ、噛むほどに口の中でアナゴの旨みと混ざり合い、味が2倍3倍と膨らんでいくように感じます。

Sushi Suzuki, Ginza

神無月 第4貫

サバの棒寿司
Saba Bo-Zushi (Rod-Shaped Mackerel Sushi)

白板昆布の甘さがアクセント

サバの棒寿司というと、関西の押し寿司やバッテラを思い浮かべる人が多いと思いますが、実は江戸前寿司でも明治時代以前から棒寿司を作っていました。ただし関西の棒寿司がシャリを押し固めて空気を抜くのに対し、江戸前は巻き簾でふんわりと巻き、空気を残します。そしてサバの酢じめも関西に比べて浅いという違いがあります。
「うちの場合、かなり浅めにしめるので、品質のいいサバを選んで使います。産地は兵庫県の淡路か神奈川県の松輪。どちらも1本釣りのサバで鮮度が抜群にいいんです」
鈴木さんはもうひとつ、サバの大きさも大事だと言います。
「大きいサバは見た目は立派でも脂がない場合が多い。ベストは700〜800グラムくらい。このサイズが一番脂のバランスがよくて、棒寿司に合います」
甘酢に浸した白板昆布を厚く切ったサバの上に乗せるのが『鮨 鈴木』のスタイル。白板昆布の優しい甘さがアクセントとなり、秋サバの濃厚な旨みを引き立てます。

Mild sweetness of shiroita-kombu as an accent

Most may imagine oshi-zushi or battera (kinds of pressed sushi) of Kansai area from the name "saba bo-zushi" (rod-shaped mackerel sushi) but bo-zushi has also existed in Edomae sushi before the Meiji Period.
To make Kansai style bo-zushi, sushi rice is pressed hard in a particular wooden box while the Edomae is rolled softly with makisu (thin mat woven from bamboo and string) to leave some air inside. Also, saba is less flavored than Kansai style.
"The quality and freshness of saba is very important because the fish is very lightly cured for bo-zushi. They are from Awaji in Hyogo Prefecture or Matsuwa in Kanagawa Prefecture, both caught by pole-and-line and very fresh."
Mr. Suzuki says the size of saba is another important factor.
"Larger saba may look wonderful but tends to have no fat. Best size is about 700 to 800 grams, very balanced amount of fat good for bo-zushi."
It is Sushi Suzuki style of bo-zushi to put sweet and sour flavored shiroita-kombu (kelp with its surface scraped off until paper thin) on thickly sliced saba. The gentle sweetness of shiroita-kombu becomes a nice accent and brings out the deep flavor of the autumn saba.

神無月 第5貫

タイラ貝
Tairagai (Japanese Pen Shell)

飴色がかっているものが旨い

タイラ貝はその名の通り平らな形をした貝で『タイラギ』とも呼ばれます。貝殻の幅は30センチ前後もあり食用の二枚貝としては大型ですが、江戸前寿司で握るのはひとつしかない貝柱の部分だけ。なので貝の中でもアワビ、ミル貝に並ぶ高級品です。
「貝柱の見た目はホタテに似ていますが、もっと旨みが強い。サクッとした食感の良さもホタテ以上。タイラ貝のよしあしは貝柱の色で見極めます。白いものより飴色がかっている方が味が濃くて旨い。今日のは愛知県三河産ですが、いい色をしています」
タイラ貝はそのまま握るのが一般的ですが、鈴木さんはシャリとの間に小さく切った海苔を挟みます。
「タイラ貝はすべって握りにくいので海苔がストッパーの役割になります。そしてタイラ貝と海苔は味の相性が抜群にいい。もっちりしたタイラ貝に海苔と煮切りが加わると、磯辺焼きのような日本人好みの味になるんです」

The amber-colored delight

Tairagai (Japanese pen shell) means "flat shells" from the way the shells actually look, also known as "tairagi". The width of the shell is up to around 30 centimeters, which is big for edible bivalves. The adductor, found only one in each shell, is used for sushi, which makes tairagai one of the most precious sushi ingredients along with awabi (abalone) or mirugai (horse clam).
"The adductor looks like hotate (scallop) but has stronger taste and crispier texture. The color of adductor tells the quality of tairagai. The amber-colored have better, stronger taste than the white ones. Today we have tairagai from Mikawa in Aichi Prefecture and the color is looking good."
The way Mr. Suzuki makes nigiri of tairagai is unique, putting tiny pieces of seaweed in between.
"Seaweed keeps tairagai from slipping in the hand when making nigiri sushi. Also, tairagai and seaweed together make an outstanding harmony of taste. The combination of chewy tairagai, seaweed, and nikiri (sweet soy sauce) tastes like isobeyaki, grilled rice cake flavored with sweet soy sauce and wrapped in seaweed, one of the most popular traditional Japanese snacks."

神無月のマグロ（砂ずり）
October Tuna (Sunazuri)

Rich and mellow

This day the master of Sushi Suzuki in Ginza, Mr. Takahisa Suzuki, had a block of "harakami" (extra fatty part on the abdomen near the gills).
"This is 'harakami' of a 165-kilo maguro (bluefin tuna). I personally believe maguro about 150 kilograms is the best as for both taste and aroma. So this one is almost the ideal size."
Maguro is a migratory fish, which moves up north following blue-skinned fish such as iwashi (sardine) and reaches the Tsugaru Strait in the autumn. The taste of the meat then changes by feeding on surume-ika (Japanese flying squid) there.
"The quality of the fat also changes as well as the taste. I can feel the change by the touch of a finger. Unlike summer maguro, the fat melts easily by the heat of the hand so I am very careful when handling otoro," says Mr. Suzuki as he cautiously slices the best part of otoro, "sunazuri", also called "jabara" meaning the belly of the snake from the way it looks with layers of white tendon and the flesh.
"White tendons of high quality maguro like this one should not be disturbing at all in the mouth, so I wouldn't remove them when making nigiri."
The natural flavor of maguro and a faint aroma of squid viscera make rich and mellow taste to cover the tongue together with melting fat.

濃密にして芳醇な味わい

銀座『鮨 鈴木』の親方・鈴木孝尚さんがこの日仕入れたのは、青森県大間産のホンマグロの"腹カミ"ブロックです。
「これは165キロのマグロの"腹カミ"。人によって好みはありますが、僕は150キロ前後のものが味も香りもベストだと思ってます。だからほぼ理想に近いサイズですね」
マグロは回遊魚で、餌であるイワシなどの青魚を追って北上し、秋に津軽海峡に到達します。そこで海域に生息するスルメイカを餌にすることで、味が変化すると言われています。
「味もそうですが、脂の質も変わる。指先で触れただけでわかります。夏のマグロと違って手の温度ですぐに脂が融けてしまうんですよ。だから大トロの扱いには気をつかいます」
そう言いながら鈴木さんが慎重に切りつけたのは、大トロの中の大トロとされる"砂ずり"。身と脂肪の白い筋が層になっている部位です。
「このクラスのマグロになると、白い筋が歯に当たることはありません。なので、筋もそのまま握ります」
握りを口に入れれば、マグロ本来のコクのある旨みにスルメイカのワタの旨みが加わった濃密な味わいが、融けた脂と共に舌を覆い尽くします。

Sushi Suzuki, Ginza

銀座 『鮨 鈴木』

銀座でもトップクラスの魚を揃えていることで知られる人気店。親方の鈴木孝尚さんは名店『鮨青木』で12年間修業し、西麻布店の店長も経験した手練の職人。ことに握る姿勢と握りの形の美しさは若手職人の中でも群を抜く。

住所：東京都中央区銀座 6-5-15　銀座能楽堂ビル 5F
電話：03-5537-6868（完全予約制）
営業時間：【昼】12：00～14：00
　　　　　【夜】18：00～22：00（閉店）
定休日：月曜日

Sushi Suzuki, Ginza

One of the most popular sushi restaurants in Ginza known for the selection of top class fish. The master, Mr. Takahisa Suzuki, is a true artisan who had trained at the famous Sushi Aoki for twelve years and has experience as a manager at the branch in Nishi-azabu. His beautiful work of nigiri sushi is beyond the league.

Address：Ginza-Nougakudo Building 5F, 6-5-15, Ginza, Chuo-ku, Tokyo
Tel：03-5537-6868（By appointment only）
Open：【lunch】12：00～14：00
　　　【dinner】18：00～22：00（close）
Closed：Mondays

霜月 [11月] の寿司
About Sushi in November
寿司だねの特徴

秋の魚に加え、冬の魚が登場してくる11月は寿司だねのラインナップが充実する時。赤貝やミル貝が登場し、ヒラメが旬を迎え、クエやハタなど大型の魚にも脂がのってきます。中でもこの時期最も旨いとされるのがヒラスズキ。旨みも脂の甘みも白身魚のトップクラスですが、漁獲が少ないため、滅多に食べられない"幻の味"となりつつあります。
そして11月の初旬には、食通たちの垂涎の的である日本海のズワイガニ（越前ガニ、松葉ガニ）の漁が始まります。江戸前寿司の老舗でズワイガニを握る店は数少ないのですが、酒肴としては人気が高く、若手を中心に使う店が増えてきました。

NOVEMBER

There are a wide variety of sushi ingredients in November when you can enjoy both autumn and winter fish. Akagai (ark shell) and mirugai (horse clam) begin to appear on sushi menus and it is the best season for hirame (Japanese flatfish). Large fish such as kue (longtooth grouper) and hata (grouper) become nice and fatty. Above all, hirasuzuki (blackfin seabass) is said to be the most delicious fish during this season. It has top-class taste and sweet fat among white fish, although you are lucky if you ever have a chance to taste it since the catch is so small that it has become a "phantom fish".
Also, the fishing season for the popular zuwaigani (snow crab) starts in the Sea of Japan at the beginning of November. There are only a few traditional Edomae sushi restaurants that serve zuwaigani as nigiri sushi but more chefs of younger generation serve them as small side dish to enjoy with sake.

Kizushi, Ningyo-cho

アナゴ
Anago (Sea Eel)

The quality shows from preparation

Anago (sea eel), along with maguro (tuna) and kohada (medium-sized konoshiro gizzard shad), is one of the classic ingredients of Edomae sushi. The quality of "Edomae anago" caught offshore of Haneda in Tokyo Bay has long been among the best throughout Japan. Nowadays, however, more restaurants prefer using anago from Tsushima in Nagasaki Prefecture.

"The best season of Edomae anago is only around the summer but the quality of anago from Tsushima is high and stable throughout the year. So I purchase anago from Tsushima in the autumn."

Anago is caught in the relatively shallow waters in Tokyo Bay while in Tsushima the fishing area is 150 to 200 meters deep where the temperature is stable as well as the condition of the fish.

"Good anago is different from the preparation. If I can easily cut the meat without knife getting stuck at the backbone, or if the meat feels as if dancing in my fingers upon rubbing with salt, I know the fish is good. I'm lucky to have such anago here today. This is from Tsushima and I could say it may be the best this season."

At Kizushi, nigiri of anago is made with the finest anago simmered until fluffy soft, served with nitsume, specially made thick sweet soy sauce. This nitsume stands out among other restaurants and there is a good reason why.

"When simmering, I also add broth of both kombu (kelp) and katsuo (bonito), and some vegetables like carrots and Japanese radish, not just the bones and heads of anago like ordinary nitsume sauce. It takes two endearing days to make the sauce but I cannot cut corners when I think of my guests telling me that the best anago is here."

旨いアナゴは仕込みの時にわかる

アナゴはマグロ、コハダと共に江戸前寿司を代表する寿司だね。それは古くから東京湾の羽田沖で獲れる"江戸前アナゴ"の品質が全国有数とされてきたからです。しかし最近は、東京湾よりも長崎県の対馬で獲れるアナゴを使う店が増えています。

「江戸前アナゴの旬は梅雨から夏にかけての一時期だけですし、個体差も大きい。それに対して対馬のアナゴは、時期によるムラが少なく一定してレベルが高いから使いやすい。だから秋は対馬産を仕入れることが多いですね」

東京湾のアナゴは比較的浅い海域で獲れますが、対馬のアナゴの漁場は水深が150〜200メートルと深く、水温の変化が少ないので、コンディションが安定していると考えられています。

「旨いアナゴは仕込みの時にわかります。捌く時、中骨に包丁がひっかからないし、塩で揉むと身が踊るような感触がある。今日のアナゴがまさにそれです。これも対馬産ですが、今期一番と言ってもいいくらいじゃないかな」

その極上のアナゴを熟練の技でふっくらと煮上げ、上から濃厚な煮ツメをたっぷりつけて出すのが『㐂寿司』の握り。この煮ツメも他店とは一線を画す味わいなのですが、それには理由があります。

「アナゴの骨や頭だけでなく、昆布だしや鰹節のだし、そして人参や大根など野菜も入れて煮詰めるんです。丸2日かかる地道な作業ですが、『アナゴは㐂寿司に限る』とおっしゃるお客さんも多いので、一切手は抜けません」

霜月　第2貫

カジキ （マカジキ） Kajiki (Striped Marlin)

Melts like fatty otoro of maguro

In the world of Edomae sushi kajiki signifies "makajiki" (striped marlin). There are various kinds of kajiki (swordfish) in the seas around Japan such as mekajiki (swordfish) and basho-kajiki (sailfish) but the most delicious is makajiki. Makajiki used to be valued higher than tuna for the mild fat and elegant taste.
"Kajiki is one of the standard sushi ingredients at my restaurant. I use the belly part called 'haramo' for nigiri, where the quality of the fat is extremely high. How it melts in the mouth may be better than fatty otoro of tuna. The peak season is from the end of December to January, so November is just the beginning of the season. Even so the fat is good enough."
At Kizushi thick slices of fatty haramo is used for nigiri. It fills up the mouth but melts in a second due to the low melting temperature.
"There aren't many restaurants that serve nigiri of kajiki but I'd strongly recommend you try. You'd see that kajiki is as delicious as the finest tuna."

脂の口どけはマグロの大トロ以上

江戸前寿司の世界でカジキと言えば"マカジキ"のこと。日本近海にはメカジキ、バショウカジキなど数種類のカジキが生息していますが、最も美味なのがマカジキです。脂がさらりとして上品な味わいであることから、戦前まではマグロより高い評価を受ける高級な寿司だねでした。
「カジキは昔からうちの定番のたね。握るのは"ハラモ"と呼ばれる腹の身で、とにかく脂の質が高い。口どけの良さならマグロの大トロ以上ではないでしょうか。年末から年明けにかけてが旬の最盛期で、11月は走りというところですが、それでも脂は十分にのっています」
脂ののったハラモを厚く切りつけて握るのが『㐂寿司』の伝統。食べると口いっぱいになりますが、脂の融点が低いので、あっという間に蕩けてしまいます。
「今、カジキを握る店は少ないですが、是非食べてみてほしい。そしてカジキが最高級のマグロにも負けないくらい旨い魚だということを知っていただけたらと思います」

霜月　第3貫

スミイカ Sumi-Ika (Japanese Spineless Cuttlefish)

Enjoy the fresh and crisp texture

Sumi-ika (Japanese spineless cuttlefish) is the name used only in the Kanto area including Tokyo, and otherwise known as "kou-ika" throughout Japan. Sumi-ika is one of the essential ingredients for Edomae cuisine, not only for sushi but tempura as well. Especially shin-ika (baby cuttlefish) seen from summer to early autumn is favored by Tokyoites who always love the first catch of the season.
"Sumi-ika has great texture, fresh and crisp. This texture may be the reason why Tokyoites love it so much. I hear more sushi masters use shiro-ika (swordtip squid) but the sticky texture isn't for Edomae style. I'd definitely prefer sumi-ika in the autumn."
This day the master had fairly big-sized sumi-ika from Koshiba in Kanagawa Prefecture, 700 grams each.
"They are rare and difficult to get at fish markets but I think those from Koshiba is the best in the country. The flesh is thick and sweet. The texture is so good elderlies can eat easily as well."

スカッとした歯切れの良さを楽しむ

スミイカは東京を含めた関東地方での呼び名で、全国的にはコウイカの名前で知られています。江戸前の料理には欠かせない食材で、寿司だけでなく天ぷらのたねとしても定番。とりわけ夏から初秋にかけて出回る新イカ（子供のイカ）は、初物好きの江戸っ子に愛されています。
「スミイカの魅力はスカッとした歯切れの良さ。それが江戸っ子の好みに合うんじゃないでしょうか。最近はスミイカの旬の時期でもシロイカを使う寿司屋が増えていると聞きますが、あのねっちりした食感は江戸前寿司らしくないと思います」
この日親方が仕入れたのは神奈川県小柴産のスミイカ。1パイ700グラムとかなり大きめなサイズです。
「入荷する数が少なくて手に入りにくいのですが、小柴は全国の産地の中でも一番だと思います。身に厚みがあって甘みが強く、これぞスミイカという味がします。歯切れの良さも絶品で、お年寄りでもサクッと食べられます」

Kizushi, Ningyo-cho

霜月　第4貫

サバ
Saba (Mackerel)

The "kurakake" style

Saba (mackerel) used to be a low-priced, common fish for the Japanese. However, those sent directly from local fisheries such as "Seki-saba" from Oita, "Misaki-saba" from Ehime, and "Kinka-saba" from Miyagi are now highly valued as brand saba to have become one of the high rank fishes.
"There are saba from all around Japan at the market but they have all different taste and texture depending on where they are from. Firm meat may be good for sashimi but tender meat is for nigiri. The closest to my ideal is from the Tohoku region. Today I got saba from Aomori."
At Kizushi, the master slices saba into thick pieces and makes them look like the shape of horse saddle, a style of nigiri sushi called "kurakake". So it is important the meat of saba is soft to go with the rice for the perfect harmony.
"Our lineup of sushi ingredients rotates fast. We serve saba only in the autumn and not after December, so it is our tradition to make nigiri with bigger slices of saba for the guests to fully enjoy the season."
When the mouth is filled with a big piece of saba, you would be hit by a wave of fine savor and sweet fat. That is a special seasonal experience only at Kizushi.

厚く切りつけ "鞍掛け" で握る

かつては値段も安く、庶民の味として親しまれてきたサバ。それがバブル時代以降、大分県の『関サバ』や愛媛県の『岬サバ』、宮城県の『金華サバ』といった地方直送のサバがブランドとして評価され、今ではすっかり高級魚のひとつになっています。
「市場には全国各地のサバが流通してますが、実はサバは産地によって味も身の質感もけっこう違うんです。刺身なら少し固い食感でもいいけど、握りには柔らかくてしっとりとした身質のものが合う。理想に近いのは東北のサバで、今日のは青森産です」
サバを大きく厚く切りつけ、馬の鞍の形に見立てた"鞍掛け"にして握るのが『㐂寿司』のスタイル。だからサバの身が固いとシャリに馴染まず、握りの一体感が味わえないのです。
「うちは寿司だねのローテーションが早く、サバは秋のもので、年明けにはもうありません。だから季節を味わってもらうため、たっぷり"つける"のが伝統なんです」
分厚いサバを頬張るようにして食べれば、極上の旨みと脂の甘みが波のように押し寄せてきます。それは『㐂寿司』でしか味わえない秋の醍醐味です。

霜月　第5貫

戻りガツオ
Modori-Gatsuo (Bonito Returning to the South)

The enhancing savor

Katsuo (bonito) is a migratory fish. They move up north with the Kuroshio Current after growing up in the southern sea below twenty degrees north latitude and reach the offshore of Boshu from April to May every year, which Tokyoites call "hatsu-gatsuo". But those that keep on moving further north to the offshore of Sanriku and come back down south in the autumn are called "modori-gatsuo", which means "returning bonito".
The master of Kizushi at Nihombashi Ningyo-cho, Mr. Kazuhiro Yui, says the best season of modori-gatsuo is November.
"In November katsuo is in excellent condition. Nice and fatty but has fresh taste and good aroma. However, you cannot judge the quality just by the appearance so I always cut the fish to check the condition of the meat before purchasing. Today I have fresh katsuo from Katsuura in Chiba Prefecture caught by trawl line."
Trawl line fishing is a method of trolling, which keeps fish fresh by using small boat to return immediately back to the port upon catching the fish.
"As for katsuo, the taste and aroma easily deteriorate with time so freshness is the most important factor."
Truly fresh modori-gatsuo has amazing texture that softly covers the tongue with the rich flavor and aroma you can only enjoy this time of the year.

噛むほどに広がる濃厚な旨み

カツオは回遊魚。北緯20度未満の南の海で育ち、一定の大きさになると黒潮に乗って北上を始め、例年4月から5月上旬に房州沖に到達します。これを江戸っ子は"初ガツオ"と呼びます。そしてさらに三陸沖あたりまで北上し、脂肪を貯えてから秋になって南下したのが"戻りガツオ"です。
日本橋人形町『㐂寿司』の三代目親方・油井一浩さんは、戻りガツオは11月がベストだと言います。
「11月のカツオは脂がのっているのに味にクセがなく、香りもあって絶品です。ただし見た目だけでは善し悪しのわからない魚ですから、市場では必ず腹を割って（おろして）状態を確認してから買うようにしています。今日のは千葉県勝浦の引き縄のカツオで、鮮度も抜群です」
引き縄というのはトローリング漁の一種で、小さい船で漁を行い、獲ってすぐに港に帰るので魚の鮮度がよく、品質も高いとされています。
「カツオは時間が経てば経つほど味も香りも落ちてしまう。だから鮮度は最も大事なポイントなんです」
舌を包み込むようなもっちりとした食感が新鮮なカツオの証。そして噛むほどに広がる濃厚な旨みは、11月の戻りガツオならではの魅力です。

68　人形町　『㐂寿司』

霜月のマグロ（血合いギシ） November Tuna (Chiai-gishi)

The finest aroma

The most expensive portion of maguro (tuna) is the block of "harakami", the extra fatty part from the belly including special cuts of otoro (extremely fatty parts of tuna) like "jabara" and "shimofuri". While high-class sushi restaurants in Ginza compete to get this precious "harakami", the master of Kizushi at Nihombashi Ningyo-cho, Mr. Kazuhiro Yui, goes for the meat at the back of maguro.

"To me the best part of maguro is red meat rather than otoro, especially the red lean meat taken from the back is more delicious. True, otoro has sweet fat but not that rich flavor or the hint of sourness unique to red meat. And the aroma…only the meat from the back has that aroma of maguro breezing through the nose."

This day the master purchased the back meat of 133-kilo maguro from Oma in Aomori Prefecture with much fat content in the midst of the season.

"Besides red meat, I'd also recommend 'chutoro' (medium fatty meat) from the back. The fat is evenly distributed so you can enjoy both the sweetness of fat and the rich flavor of red meat. Especially the area called 'chiai-gishi' (portion near red dark meat) has excellent aroma. It must be irresistible for maguro lovers."

鼻に抜ける極上の香り

マグロの中で最も高価な部位は蛇腹や霜降りといった大トロが取れる"腹カミ"のブロック。銀座の高級店が競ってこの"腹カミ"を買い求める中、日本橋人形町『㐂寿司』の親方・油井 浩さんは、腹ではなく背の身にこだわります。

「マグロは大トロより赤身。特に背の赤身が旨い…というのがうちの信条。大トロは脂の甘みはありますけど、赤身のような旨みや酸味、コク深い味わいはない。そして香り。あの鼻に抜けるようなマグロ特有の香りは背の身ならではの魅力です」

この日仕入れたのは青森県大間産133キロのホンマグロの背の身。日本一のブランドと呼ばれる大間の、しかも旬真っ盛りのマグロですから、背とはいえ上質な脂がたっぷりのっています。

「赤身はもちろんですが、中トロも食べてほしいです。背の中トロは脂がまんべんなく入っているので、脂の甘みと赤身のコクが両方味わえます。とりわけ"血合いギシ"の部分は香りが素晴らしい。マグロ好きな人にはたまらないと思いますよ」

Kizushi, Ningyo-cho

人形町 『㐂寿司』

大正12年（1923）創業の老舗にして、江戸前寿司の元祖「輿兵衛ずし」の流れを汲む名店として、都内でもトップクラスの格式を誇る。2018年に親方を受け継いだ油井一浩さんが三代目としてつけ場に立つ。

住所：東京都中央区日本橋人形町 2-7-13
電話：03-3666-1682
営業時間：[月〜金] 11：45 〜 14：30　17：00 〜 21：30
　　　　　[土] 11：45 〜 14：30　17：00 〜 21：00
定休日：日曜日、祝日
　　　　（日曜日祝日連休の場合　日曜日　11：45 〜 14：30）

Kizushi, Ningyo-cho

One of the top class sushi restaurants in Tokyo opened back in 1923 following the tradition of Yoheizushi, the original Edomae sushi restaurant. The third generation master, Mr. Kazuhiro Yui, who took over his father in 2018 serves outstanding sushi.

Address：2-7-13, Nihombashi Ningyo-cho, Chuo-ku, Tokyo
Tel：03-3666-1682
Open：[Monday 〜 Friday] 11：45 〜 14：30　17：00 〜 21：30
　　　[Saturday] 11：45 〜 14：30　17：00 〜 21：00
Closed：Sundays & National Holidays
　　　　（Sundays and holidays【Sunday】11：45 〜 14：30）

12月は江戸前寿司の花形であるホンマグロが最も美味しくなる時。とりわけ津軽海峡のホンマグロはこの時期にスルメイカを餌にすることで上質な脂を貯え、味も香りもピークに達すると言われています。
ノドグロやサワラも美味。日本海のノドグロは脂がのって旨みを増し、サワラは魚体が大きくなって"寒ザワラ"と呼ばれるようになります。
そして12月は魚だけでなく貝類も充実しています。江戸前寿司の定番である赤貝、タイラ貝、ミル貝に加え、北寄貝やツブ貝などもこの時期が旬。カキも粒が大きくなり甘みが増します。

DECEMBER

In December hon-maguro (bluefin tuna), the king of Edomae sushi, become superbly delicious. Especially the taste and aroma of hon-maguro feeding on surume-ika (Japanese flying squid) in the Tsugaru Strait could not be more delicious with high quality fat.
Nodoguro (rosy seabass) and sawara (Spanish mackerel) are also very delicious. Nodoguro from the Sea of Japan contains much fat with richer taste, and sawara becomes larger to be called "kan-zawara" meaning the "winter sawara".
There are also a wide variety of shellfish in December. The classic akagai (ark shell), tairagai (Japanese pen shell), mirugai (horse clam), hokkigai (surf clam), and tsubugai (whelk), are all in season. Not to forget oysters become bigger and sweeter.

Sushi Namba, Asagaya

師走 第1貫

ミズダコ (Mizudako (Giant Pacific Octopus))

The more you chew, the sweeter

Mizudako (giant Pacific octopus) is the largest octopus in the world, reaches up to three meters long. It has very rich flavor and tender texture despite the size, so more restaurants prefer using mizudako nowadays. The master of Sushi Namba at Asagaya, Mr. Shunsuke Takaoka, is one of them.
"We use madako (East Asian common octopus) to make nidako (simmered octopus) but use fresh mizudako for nigiri sushi. I like the refreshing taste of mizudako and use it often in winter when other sushi ingredients are fatty and a little heavy. People have the impression that octopus is difficult to chew when raw but mizudako is very tender so you wouldn't have to worry about not being able to chew."
Nigiri of mizudako is served with just a pinch of salt and a squeeze of sudachi (a kind of Japanese citrus), which is enough for the deep flavor that spreads in the mouth.
"I really want my guests to taste the freshest so I use them within a day, or the next day at most. Guests who try mizudako for the first time are astonished at the fresh texture and taste unlikely of octopus."

噛みしめるほどに甘みが広がる

ミズダコは全長3メートルにも達するという世界最大のタコ。その大きさのわりに旨みがあり食感も柔らかいので、最近は寿司だねにする店が増えています。阿佐ヶ谷『鮨 なんば』の高岡俊輔さんもミズダコを積極的に使うひとりです。
「うちでは煮ダコにするのはマダコ、生を握るのはミズダコと使い分けています。ミズダコのさっぱりした味が好きなので、脂っこい魚の多い冬にはよく握りにします。タコは生だと固いというイメージがあるかと思いますが、ミズダコは柔らかいので大丈夫。さっくりと噛み切れます」
握りに添えるのは、わずかな塩と絞ったすだちのみ。それでも噛みしめるほどに深い旨みが舌に広がります。
「新鮮なうちに食べてほしいので、仕入れたその日か翌日には使い切るようにしています。タコとは思えないフレッシュな食感と味わいに初めて食べた方は驚かれますね」

師走 第2貫

カワハギ (Kawahagi (Thread-Sail Filefish))

Rich flavor of liver like "otoro"

Kawahagi (thread-sail filefish) is a fish of the family Monacanthidae in the order Tetraodontiformes. The peculiar name, meaning "peeling off the skin", comes from the way in which the hard and thick skin of the fish is peeled off upon cooking.
Simple but sweet, the flavor is similar to fugu (pufferfish). The liver is exceptionally delicious and it is called "foie gras of the sea".
"Kawahagi has the best liver so I use them from around October when the liver become fatty but December is the best time. Today I have kawahagi from Izumi in Kagoshima Prefecture. I use kawahagi from the Kyushu area because they have firm meat and good quality liver."
As for nigiri, Mr. Takaoka does nothing to the meat but puts a big piece of liver in between the sushi rice. He does not use any condiments like scallion or chive.
"The rich and sweet taste of the liver is as good as otoro of maguro (tuna). This is why I don't add any condiments for guests to enjoy simply the taste of the fish."

肝の濃厚な旨みは
大トロに匹敵

カワハギはフグ目カワハギ科の魚。その風変わりな名前は、皮が固いため「皮を剥いで料理する」ところからつけられたもの。
淡白な味わいの中にしっかり甘みがあり、フグに似た旨みがあるのが特徴。そして肝（肝臓）の味はすべての魚のトップクラス。その美味しさから"海のフォアグラ"とも呼ばれています。
「カワハギの魅力は肝に尽きます。なので肝に脂がのる10月頃から使い始めます。でも一番いいのは12月ですね。今日のは鹿児島県出水産ですが、九州のカワハギは全体的に身が筋肉質で歯応えがよく、肝の脂の質も高いのでよく使います」
高岡さんはカワハギの身には何も手は加えず、シャリの間に大きく切った肝を挟んで握ります。香りづけのネギやアサツキも一切use用いません。
「肝の濃厚な旨み、甘みはマグロの大トロに匹敵するもの。香りづけをしないのは、その味わいをストレートに楽しんでいただきたいからです」

キハダマグロ
Kihada-Maguro (Yellowfin Tuna)

Smooth texture and excellent aroma

Kihada-maguro (yellowfin tuna) is a middle-sized tuna, which grows only up to about two meters and contains less fat compared to hon-maguro (bluefin tuna) or minami-maguro (southern bluefin tuna). The light taste is more popular in Kansai than in Tokyo and the fish is barely seen in Edomae style restaurants.
"A maguro broker recommended me to try kihada-maguro and I found out it is very attractive in a way different from hon-maguro. Soft meat, and light but rich taste. Red meat, especially, has excellent aroma."
A bite of nigiri and you would be surprised at the smooth texture and the gorgeous aroma. With not so much fat but elegant sweetness you could eat one after another.

滑らかな舌触りと華やかな香り

キハダマグロは成長しても全長2メートル程度という中型のマグロ。ホンマグロやミナミマグロより脂肪が少なく、クセのない味わいが関東より関西で好まれており、江戸前寿司の店で握ることはほとんどありません。
「マグロ屋さんにすすめられて試したのがきっかけですが、キハダにはホンマグロとは違う魅力があるんです。身にほどよい柔らかさがあって、さっぱりした味なのに旨みがしっかり感じられる。特に赤身は香りもすばらしい」
握りを口に含むと、キハダマグロの滑らかな舌触りと、鼻腔をくすぐる華やかな香りに驚きます。脂ののりはあっさりしていますが上品な甘みがあり、いくつ食べても飽きがこない味わいです。

Sushi Namba, Asagaya

師走　第4貫

北寄貝　Hokkigai (Surf Clam)

Rich and smoky flavor of grilled hokkigai

Hokkigai (surf clam) is a marine bivalve in the family Mactridae. It has long been eaten in Hokkaido and Tohoku area, but it was not until the 1990's when the technology developed to transport fresh marine products that hokkigai become one of the common ingredients for Edomae sushi.
"I have to be careful when I buy hokkigai because they live in sandy areas and often contain sand. Today I chose the best of the best, about 500 grams each including the shells. Thick meat and sweet flavor."
Upon making nigiri, hokkigai is grilled after brushing on sweet soy sauce. Unlike other chefs, Mr. Takaoka does not cut off the liver.
"The liver is often taken off to avoid the smell but it is better left on when very fresh. The liver has rich savor and becomes even more tastier when grilled, perfect to enjoy with sake."

炙って旨みと香ばしさを出す

北寄貝はバカ貝科の二枚貝。茨城県以北の太平洋と日本海北部の冷たい海に生息し、北海道や東北では昔から食べられていましたが、江戸前寿司のたねとして使われるようになったのは、流通がよくなった90年代以降と言われています。
「砂地に棲む北寄貝は砂を噛んで（含んで）いることが多いので、買う時には気をつかいます。今日のは仲買さんの選り抜きの中からさらに選んだもの。貝殻を合わせてひとつ500グラムあります。身が厚くて、甘みが強いです」
高岡さんは北寄貝のワタをあえて残し、煮切りをつけて炙ってから握ります。
「臭みが出るからとワタを取る店が多いのですが、貝の鮮度がいいので残してあります。ワタには濃厚な旨みがあり、炙ることで香ばしくなるので、日本酒と合わせるとさらに旨いです」

師走　第5貫

ノドグロ　Nodoguro (Rosy Seabass)

Adding the smoky aroma of straw

Nodoguro, meaning black throat, is the nickname used in Hokuriku and Sanin area, the coast of the Sea of Japan, and the official name is akamutsu (rosy seabass). However, the name nodoguro became more familiar nationwide as the fish often appeared in the media as "the delicacy of the Sea of Japan".
"Nodoguro is very delicious but must be fresh and not too fatty, or otherwise could smell fishy. This year they are fatty but firm and evenly in good shape. Very high quality in these few years."
At Sushi Namba, the side with the skin is seared with flame from straw to get rid of extra fat and add a deep smoky flavor.
"It is important not to grill too much for the soft texture. Also, we prepare two types of sushi rice depending on the kind of fish, white sushi rice flavored with rice vinegar and red sushi rice using red vinegar. Red sushi rice has stronger flavor and matches nodoguro."
The sweet fat of nodoguro and the savor of red sushi rice unite in the mouth and leave you speechless with the profound taste.

藁のスモーキーな香りを纏わせる

"ノドグロ"は北陸や山陰など日本海沿岸で使われてきた通称で、正式名称は『アカムツ』。でも近年は"日本海の美味"としてメディアで取り上げられる機会が増え、ノドグロの呼び名の方がポピュラーになりつつあります。
「美味しい魚ですが、脂がのりすぎていたり鮮度が悪いとクセが出てしまうのがノドグロの特徴。でもこの冬のノドグロは脂がのっていても身がゆるくないし、魚によるバラつきも少ない。すごくレベルが高いと思います」
ノドグロの皮目を藁の火で炙って余分な脂を落とし、スモーキーな香りを纏わせるのが『鮨 なんば』のスタイル。
「ふんわりした食感にするため、炙る時に必要以上に火を入れないのがポイントです。うちは白と赤、2種類のシャリを魚によって使い分けますが、ノドグロには旨みの強い赤シャリを合わせます」
握りを食べればノドグロの甘い脂と赤シャリの旨みが口の中でひとつになり、唸るような深い味わいへと変わります。

阿佐ヶ谷　『鮨 なんば　阿佐ヶ谷』

師走のマグロ（腹シタの中トロ）
December Tuna (Chutoro of Harashita)

An explosion of the taste

The best time to enjoy maguro (tuna) is December when they contain much fat by the decrease of the sea temperature. Best sushi restaurants compete for the top class maguro.
"Today we have 260-kilo hon-maguro from Toi in Hokkaido. It's the perfect winter maguro with the best aroma, sourness, and fat," says Mr. Shunsuke Takaoka of Sushi Namba with confidence.
"This is a cut called 'harashita'. It is a part of meat on the abdomen a little close to the tail, where red meat and fat are nicely balanced with both two different flavors. It has been well matured for two weeks so I'm sure the taste would explode in the mouth."
The size of each slice of chutoro (medium fatty part of tuna) is fairly big for nigiri so that the guests can enjoy the true taste of maguro. The aroma, the rich and deep savor, and the sweetness of the fat that only the top class maguro has, all dance at once on the tongue like an explosion.

最高のマグロの爆発的な旨み

海水温が下がり身にたっぷりと脂を貯えた12月はマグロが一年中で最も美味しい時。名店と呼ばれる寿司屋は、その中でもさらにトップクラスのマグロを手に入れるために競います。
「今日のは北海道戸井産ホンマグロの260キロ。香り、酸味、脂ののり、すべてが申し分のない"THE 冬のマグロ"です」
そう言い切る『鮨 なんば』の高岡俊輔さんの顔には、自信が満ち溢れています。
「これは"腹シタ"という部位。やや尾に近い腹の身ですが、赤身とトロのバランスがよく、両方の旨みを併せ持っています。2週間ほど寝かせてしっかり熟成させているので、食べたら旨みが口の中で爆発すると思いますよ」
味がよくわかるようにと大きく厚く切りつけた中トロを口に入れると、最高クラスのマグロだけが持つ香り、旨み、コク、そして脂の甘みがいっぺんに舌の上で踊り出します。それはまさに"爆発的"な美味しさです。

Sushi Namba, Asagaya

阿佐ヶ谷
『鮨 なんば　阿佐ヶ谷』

他店の追随を許さない圧倒的なコストパフォーマンスで、3ヶ月以上先まで予約が取れないという都内屈指の人気店。親方の難波英史さんが2018年に日比谷店に移ったため、若き俊英・高岡俊輔さんがつけ場に立っている。

住所：東京都杉並区阿佐谷南 3-44-4 B1F
電話：03-3391-3118
営業時間：18：00〜20：50
　　　　　21：00〜24：00（二部制）
定休日：水曜日

Sushi Namba, Asagaya

One of the most popular restaurants in Tokyo with exceptional cost performance and three months waiting list. The master, Mr. Hidefumi Namba, moved to another branch restaurant in Hibiya, so now young and talented Mr. Shunsuke Takaoka is in charge at Asagaya.

Address：B1, 3-44-4, Asagaya-Minami, Suginami-ku, Tokyo
Tel：03-3391-3118
Open：【2 rotation system】① 18：00〜20：50　② 21：00〜24：00
Closed：Wednesdays

寿司用語

【シャリ】

すし飯のこと。その語源は仏舎利（お釈迦さまの遺骨）から来ているとも、米を洗う時にシャリシャリと音がするからとも言われ、定説はない。江戸前寿司では炊いた米に米酢、塩、砂糖を混ぜた"合わせ酢"で味をつけるのが一般的。ただしシャリに砂糖を入れるようになったのは戦後のことで、戦前までは米酢ではなく酒粕を原料にした赤酢を使い、塩のみで味つけをしていた。近年は若手の鮨職人の間でこの赤酢のシャリが再評価され、使う店が増えている。赤酢には米酢にはない独特の旨みがあり、それが魚の味を引き立てると言われている。

[Shari]

Vinegared rice cooked and seasoned for sushi. It is said that the word "shari" originally came from "busshari", meaning the remains of Buddha, or referred to the sound "shari, shari" (crunching sound) as stirring rice grains in the water to wash them before cooking, but there is no established theory. Generally, in Edomae sushi, cooked rice is flavored with "awase-zu", mixture of rice vinegar, salt, and sugar. However, using sugar was not common before 1940's, and until then, red vinegar made from sakekasu (lees left over from sake production) was used instead of rice vinegar and only salt is added. Young generation of sushi masters is revaluating red vinegar and many take in this old style of making sushi rice. It has a unique taste rice vinegar does not have to bring out the best in each piece of fish.

【煮切り】

握りに塗るために調味した醤油。「煮切り醤油」の略語。濃口醤油に日本酒、味醂、かつおだしなどを加え、鍋でひと煮立ちさせて作る。加熱して日本酒や味醂のアルコール分を飛ばすことを「煮切る」ということからこの名がある。江戸前寿司ではこれを小さなハケで握りに塗って出すのが伝統的なスタイル。

[Nikiri]

A name for soy sauce prepared especially for sushi. Abbreviated word for "nikiri-shoyu". Made by boiling, just for a few seconds, condensed soy sauce, sake, mirin (sweet sake used to add flavor), fish broth, and sometimes more ingredients. The word comes from the verb "nikiru" which means "to heat alcohol out of sake and mirin". Putting "nikiri" on top of sushi with a small brush as a finishing touch is the traditional way of serving Edomae sushi.

【煮ツメ】

アナゴなどにつける甘ダレのこと。基本的にはアナゴの煮汁にアナゴの中骨から取っただしを加え、砂糖（またはザラメ）と日本酒を入れ、とろ火で煮詰めて作るが、ごく一部にイカなど他の魚介の煮汁を加えて煮詰めるという店もある。またハマグリ専用にハマグリの茹で汁で作った煮ツメのことを"ハマツメ"と呼ぶ。江戸前寿司の老舗には、古い煮ツメに新しい煮ツメを注ぎ足しながら何十年も使い続けている所があり、こうした煮ツメは年代物として珍重される。

[Nitsume]

Sweet sauce used for sushi ingredients such as anago (sea eel). Basically "nitsume" is made from the broth used to simmer anago, the stock from the backbone, sugar (or crystalized sugar), and sake, simmered until it becomes a thick sauce. There are some sushi restaurants where they add the broth of squid. Nitsume made from water used to boil hamaguri (hard clams) is called "hamatsume" and used just for hamaguri. Some of the long-established Edomae sushi restaurants use aged nitsume for many years by adding fresh nitsume little by litte, and these nitsume are considered very precious.

【トロ】

マグロの脂肪の多い身の総称（最近はマグロ以外の魚にも用いられることがある）。元々は単に脂身と呼ばれていたが、大正時代に日本橋『吉野鮨本店』の常連客が「口の中でとろける」ことから"トロ"と呼び、それが広まったというのが有力な説とされている。老若男女問わず、最も人気の高い寿司だねである。

[Toro]

General term for the fatty part of maguro (tuna), also used for other fish nowadays. Originally, it was just called the "fatty meat", but it is said that a patron of a sushi restaurant, Yoshinosushi at Nihombashi, called it "toro" from how it "toro-keru" (melts) in the mouth in the Taisho period and the name has spread to become the common name. The most popular sushi ingredient for all generations.

【中トロ】

大トロに次いで脂の多い部分。腹側の身から取れる中トロは大トロに近いものから赤身に近いものまで幅があり、背側の中トロは全体に均一に脂がのっているものが多い。背側の中トロの中で特に質の高いものは『背トロ』と呼ばれ、大トロと同等の扱いを受ける。

[Chutoro]

Medium fatty part of maguro (tuna). The belly side of chutoro varies from otoro-like extra fatty part to less fatty part almost like red meat while chutoro on the back is evenly fatty. Especially high quality chutoro on the back is called "setoro" and classified as the same rank as the precious otoro.

【大トロ】

天然マグロのトロ全体の中で2割程度しかない、特に脂肪の多い部分のこと。脂肪が牛肉の霜降りのように散らばっているものを『霜降り』。白い脂肪の筋が蛇腹状に入ったものを『蛇腹』と呼ぶ。またカマ下（エラの下の部位）にある『カマトロ』も大トロと呼ばれることがある。

[Otoro]

Especially fatty part of wild maguro (tuna), only 20 percent of all the toro meat. Those with marbled fat similar to beef are called "shimofuri", which translates as "fallen frost", and it is called "jabara" if the lines of white fat look like the belly of a snake. Also "kama-toro" found below the gills of maguro is classified as a kind of otoro.

【米酢】

米を主原料として醸造するお酢のこと。クセの少ないまろやかな味わいで、なおかつ米の風味があることから寿司に合うとされ、シャリ（すし飯）の合わせ酢に用いられる。100パーセント米のみを原料とするものは『純米酢』と呼ばれる。

[Komezu]

Vinegar made mainly from fermented rice. It is mild yet maintains the flavor of rice and said to be the best matching vinegar for shari (sushi rice). Those made only from rice are called "junmai-su" (pure rice vinegar).

【白シャリ】

米酢をベースに味つけしたシャリ（すし飯）の通称。赤酢を用いたシャリに比べて色が薄いので "白シャリ" と呼ばれる。酢の酸味を抑えるため砂糖を入れることが多く、甘みがあるので、コハダのような塩でしめた魚や、ヒラメやカレイといった繊細な味の白身魚と合うとされる。

[Shiro-shari]

General name for shari (sushi rice) flavored with rice vinegar based seasoning. It is called "shiro-shari" (white rice) in comparison with shari flavored with red vinegar. Sugar is often added to reduce the sourness of vinegar so it goes well with salt-matured fish like kohada (medium-sized konoshiro gizzard shad) and white fish with delicate taste such as hirame (Japanese flatfish) or karei (flounder).

【赤酢】

米ではなく日本酒の醸造工程でできる酒粕を長期熟成させて作った酢のこと。江戸時代からシャリ用の酢として使われてきた。熟成させた酒粕には百種類以上のアミノ酸が含まれているため、米酢より格段に旨みが強いのが特徴。

[Akazu]

Vinegar made by fermenting not rice but sake lees for a long time. Akazu has been used for sushi rice since the Edo period. Fermented sake lees contain more than a hundred kinds of amino acid and the flavor is stronger than rice vinegar.

【赤シャリ】

赤酢をベースに味つけしたシャリのこと。江戸時代から戦前までにはこれが江戸前寿司のスタンダードだった。香りにクセがあるが、白シャリより旨み成分が多くマグロなどの赤身魚と相性がいいので、近年再評価されている。

[Aka-shari]

Shari (sushi rice) flavored with akazu-based seasoning. Aka-shari was the standard sushi rice in Edomae sushi from the Edo period to the 1940's. It has unique aroma but is highly valued in the recent years for the complicated taste that goes well with red meat fish like maguro.

【あがり】

寿司屋で供される熱い緑茶のこと。手早くたくさんの量を抽出するため、高級な煎茶ではなく粉茶（煎茶を製造する過程で出た粉状の茶葉）を使うのが一般的。"あがり" という呼称は、花柳界の符丁でお茶のことを「上がり花」と言ったことに由来する。

[Agari]

Hot green tea served at sushi restaurants. Generally powder tea left from the production of sencha (ordinary green leaf tea) is used instead of high quality leaf tea to prepare liters quickly. The term "agari" came from the word "agari-bana" meaning Japanese tea used in the world of Geisha.

【おまかせ】

注文するメニューをお店の側に任せること。高級な寿司屋のほとんどで採用されているシステムで、席に着いて「おまかせで」と言えば、コース料理のように握りとおつまみが順番に出てくる（握りのみを提供する店もある）。客側がメニューの内容を変えることはできないが、苦手な食材を予め伝えておけば、それを出さないように配慮してくれる。

[Omakase]

To leave what you eat up to the chef. Most of high-rank sushi restaurants follow this "omakase" style. Just by asking for "omakase" after taking your seat, nigiri (hand-pressed) sushi and side dishes are served like a course menu. Some restaurants only serve nigiri sushi. Guests cannot change the lineup of omakase menu but you can let master know your dislikes in advance.

【おきまり】

寿司屋で用意している握り一人前のセットメニューのこと。握り10カン前後で構成され、内容に応じて「松」「竹」「梅」といったランクづけがされているが、握りをランダムに注文する "お好み" より値段は安く設定されている。かつては江戸前寿司のほとんどの店にあったが、現在は一部の店にしか存在しないので注意が必要。

[Okimari]

A fixed set of nigiri sushi for one person served at sushi restaurants. Consists of about ten nigiri, often ranked in three grades as "matsu" (pine), "take" (bamboo), and "ume" (plum). The price is lower than "okonomi", where the guests order nigiri at random. Most sushi restaurants had okimari, but nowadays only a few have it so you need to be careful.

【お好み】

「おまかせ」でも「おきまり」でもなく、客が自分の好きな寿司だねを選び、好きな順番で注文すること。20年ほど前まではこのスタイルがスタンダードだったが、おまかせが中心となってしまった現在は、お好みで注文できる店そのものが減少している。

[Okonomi]

A style of serving sushi, neither "omakase" (up to the chef style) nor "okimari" (fixed set), in which the guests choose sushi ingredients they prefer and order in however order they like. This was the standard style until about 20 years ago although rarely seen now that omakase has become more popular.

【本わさび】

魚の生臭みを消し、味にアクセントを与える、江戸前寿司には欠かせない調味料。アブラナ科ワサビ属の植物で、地下茎の部分をすりおろし、寿司だねに適量をつけて用いる。近縁種のセイヨウワサビ（ホースラディッシュ）や加工品の粉わさびと区別するために "本わさび" と呼ぶ。水質のいい渓流や湧水を利用して栽培される "水わさび" が味も香りも最上とされる。

[Honwasabi]

A condiment indispensable for Edomae sushi used to reduce fishiness and give accent to the taste. It is a plant of the Eutrema genus of the Brassicaceae family and the stem is grated before putting on ingredients for sushi. It is called "honwasabi" (real wasabi) to distinguish from horseradish and processed powder wasabi. A kind called "mizuwasabi" (water wasabi) grown by clear mountain streams or using spring water is famous for the best aroma and the taste.

【ちらしずし】

シャリに数種類の寿司だねを乗せる、あるいは混ぜて作る寿司の一種。シャリの上（または中）に寿司だねを"散らして"作ることからこの名がついた。江戸前寿司では酢じめのコハダ、茹でたエビ、煮たアナゴなど、調理したたねを細かく切って散らしたものを『ばらちらし』、生の魚を使うものを『生ちらし』と呼んで区別している。

[Chirashi-zushi]

A type of sushi made by decorating several kinds of ingredients on top of sushi rice, or mixing ingredients with the rice. "Chirashi" literally means "scattered", and this is where the name came from as variety of ingredients are "scattered" on rice. In Edomae sushi, prepared ingredients such as vinegared kohada (medeium-sized konoshiro gizzard shad), boiled shrimp, simmered anago (sea eel), chopped and spread on sushi rice is called "bara-chirashi", and when raw fish is used it is distinguished by calling "nama-chirashi".

【細巻】

巻き寿司の中で、直径３センチ程度の口に入れやすい大きさのものの呼称。その見た目から鉄砲巻とも呼ばれる。江戸前寿司で最もポピュラーなのは甘辛く煮た干瓢を具にして巻く『かんぴょう巻』であり、かつては握りを食べ終えた後の締め（最後の一品）として、これを食べるのが通とされた。

[Hosomaki]

Rolled sushi of small size, about three centimeters diameter. From the way they look, sometimes called "teppo maki" (gun roll). The most popular of these small rolls in Edomae sushi is "kanpyo maki" which dried strips of gourd are flavored with soy sauce and sugar, and then rolled inside sushi rice. It used to be the traditional style to conclude sushi course with kanpyo maki.

【ガリ】

皮を剥いた生姜を薄く切り、甘酢漬けにしたもの。生姜のさっぱりした香りと辛味が魚の生臭みを消してくれることから、口直しとして用いられる。最近は薄切りでなくぶつ切りにしたり、砂糖を使わない辛口のガリも増えている。食べる時にガリガリと音がすることがその語源とされている。

[Gari]

Pickled ginger. Ginger is peeled, sliced, and pickled in sweetened vinegar. Fresh and spicy flavor of ginger eliminates fishy smell so it is served with sushi to refresh your mouth. These days there are more unique types, not sliced but cut in small cubes or unsweetened, for example. The name "gari" is said to be from the expression "gari gari", the sound of biting in Japanese.

【光りもの】

コハダ、アジ、サバ、サヨリなど、皮が銀白色に光って見える魚のこと。背中が青みを帯びて見える"青魚"と混同されることが多いが、江戸前寿司ではキスやカスゴなど青魚の範疇には入らない魚も光りものと呼ぶ。白身魚などと比べて鮮度が落ちるのが早い魚が多いため、古くから酢じめという技法で鮮度の低下を防いでいた。今もコハダやサバには酢じめを施すのが一般的。

[Hikarimono]

Silver-white skinned fish such as kohada (gizzard shad), aji (mackerel), and sayori (Japanese halfbeak). Often confused with "blue fish" with bluish color at its back but in Edomae sushi, those not categorized as "blue fish" like kisu (Japanese whiting) and kasugo (baby sea bream) are also included. Since most of which tend to lose freshness faster than white fish, for example, a technique sujime (curing with vinegar) has been used traditionally to keep fresh. Still now sujime is generally applied for kohada and saba.

【昆布じめ】

ヒラメやスズキといった白身魚や、甘エビや白エビ、ホタルイカなど淡白な味の魚介に昆布の旨み（グルタミン酸など）をプラスするための技。食材を昆布で挟んで数時間から数日寝かせて味を移す。乾燥した昆布には魚介の水分を吸う作用もあるため、水っぽい味を引き締めるためにも使われる。

[Kobujime]

A technique to add "umami" (tasty flavor) of kombu (kelp), such as glutamic acid, to fish and shellfish with simple taste. Used for white meat fish like hirame (Japanese flatfish) and suzuki (Japanese sea bass), or ama-ebi (sweet shrimp), shiro-ebi (Japanese glass shrimp), and hotaru-ika (firefly squid). Ingredients are wrapped with kombu and let stand for a few hours to a few days until the flavor is transferred. Dried kombu absorbs the moisture of fish so it is also used to sharpen watery taste of the ingredients.

【酢じめ】

酢の持つ殺菌、臭い消しの効果を利用して、生魚の鮮度の低下を防ぎ、生臭みやクセを抑えるための技法。いきなり酢につけると魚がふやけ、味がぼやけてしまうので、まず魚の表面に塩を振り、浸透圧で余分な水分を取り除いてから酢に浸す。浸す時間は数分から数十分で、長いほど保存性は増すが、酢の作用でタンパク質が固くなり食感が悪くなってしまうため、バランスが重要となる。

[Sujime]

A technique to keep raw fish fresh and reduce fishy smell by bactericidal, deodorizing effect of vinegar. Salting the fish is necessary before curing in vinegar. In doing so, excess moisture is removed due to osmosis. Without this process, the fish becomes soggy and tastes dull. The longer time in vinegar, the longer the conservation but as the acid coagulates proteins and changes the texture of the fish, a few minutes to about half an hour should be adequate. The balance is important.

寿司ペディア TOKYO
~ The Best 12 Affordable Sushi Restaurants in Tokyo by Hikari Hayakawa ~

2019 年 10 月 30 日　第 1 刷発行

著者	早川　光
	竹内　香苗（英訳）
発行人	松澤　肇
発行所	株式会社　ホーム社
	〒 101-0051 東京都千代田区神田神保町 3-29 共同ビル
	電話［編集部］03-5211-2651

発売元　　　株式会社　集英社
　　　　　　〒 101-8050 東京都千代田区一ツ橋 2-5-10
　　　　　　電話［販売部］03-3230-6393（書店専用）
　　　　　　　　　［読者係］03-3230-6080

印刷所　　　大日本印刷株式会社
製本所　　　加藤製本株式会社

撮影　　　　木内　章浩
　　　　　　鈴木　昭寿

編集　　　　國川　俊郎
デザイン　　志村　謙［Banana Grove Studio］

◇定価はカバーに表示してあります。
◇造本には十分注意しておりますが、乱丁・落丁（本のページ順序の間違いや抜け落ち）の場合はお取替え致します。購入された書店名を明記して集英社読者係宛にお送り下さい。送料は集英社負担でお取替え致します。但し、古書店で購入したものについてはお取替えできません。
◇本書の一部あるいは全部を無断で複写・複製することは、法律で認められた場合を除き、著作権の侵害となります。また、業者など、読者本人以外による本書のデジタル化は、いかなる場合でも一切認められませんのでご注意下さい。

©Hikari Hayakawa/Kanae Takeuchi 2019, Printed in Japan
ISBN　978-4-8342-5333-7 C0077